Dear Suzanne:

Missed you but a cruise sounds great,

Love, Peace and healing energies coming your way á

Joe Kraus

Jane Against The Grain

awakening to the mystery of life

JANE KRAMER

COAUTHOR
STEFANIE ANGSTADT

BALBOA.
PRESS
A DIVISION OF HAY HOUSE

Cover image "Awakening", oil painting by Artist Robb Kramer

Balboa Press books may be ordered through booksellers or by contacting:

Balboa Press
A Division of Hay House
1663 Liberty Drive
Bloomington, IN 47403
www.balboapress.com
1 (877) 407-4847

Because of the dynamic nature of the Internet, any web addresses or links contained in this book may have changed since publication and may no longer be valid. The views expressed in this work are solely those of the author and do not necessarily reflect the views of the publisher, and the publisher hereby disclaims any responsibility for them.

The author of this book does not dispense medical advice or prescribe the use of any technique as a form of treatment for physical, emotional, or medical problems without the advice of a physician, either directly or indirectly. The intent of the author is only to offer information of a general nature to help you in your quest for emotional and spiritual well-being. In the event you use any of the information in this book for yourself, which is your constitutional right, the author and the publisher assume no responsibility for your actions.

Any people depicted in stock imagery provided by Thinkstock are models, and such images are being used for illustrative purposes only. Certain stock imagery © Thinkstock.

Printed in the United States of America.

ISBN: 978-1-4525-2330-9 (sc)
ISBN: 978-1-4525-2329-3 (hc)
ISBN: 978-1-4525-2328-6 (e)

Library of Congress Control Number: 2014918050

Balboa Press rev. date: 10/21/2014

For my dad, Bob Woodcock and my husband,
Ted, who have not only provided me with roots,
but are truly the wind beneath my wings.

To this day, I marvel at the simplicity and effectiveness of Jane's strategy.
—Maureen Ehrlich, close friend

Contents

Foreword

by Stefanie

Drawing glances from faces across the dining room, Jane enters a posh restaurant, Lily's on Main, clad in costume. She wears an oversized white T-shirt featuring the image of a voluptuous woman, starting from the neck down, bearing a revealing string bikini. The neck of the figure is cut off where the skin of a seventy-five-year-old woman meets that of the tanned, cartoon version. Atop her silver-haired crown, she sports a massive, colorful straw hat decorated with ribbons and flowers. Over her twinkling hazel eyes, heart-shaped sunglasses serve as spectacles. She looks like she is ready for the beach.

Flanked by two of her close friends, Ellen and Mary, who are sporting matching attire, they enter the dining room without explanation for their charade. The owner has already become familiar with this crazy trio.

"Right this way, ladies," he says as he shows them to their table. They are seated, and their giddy laughter will soon engender curious glances and smiles from around the room.

As she looks back on more than fifty years, Ellen recalls the early years of her friendship with Jane:

"It was 1962 when I first met Jane. Her generous, loving spirit and Irish sense of humor were a breath of fresh air to the mild and reserved Pennsylvania German farming neighborhood. With her carefree approach to life, Jane lightened many a day and heart of the emotionally repressed, hard-working folks who knew her, and pretty soon, that was most people. The idea that there could be more notes on the German emotional piano than the standard 'fine' or 'not so gudt' (which described a state of near death) was a real awakening to our family. Gosh, you could stop working and laugh, be silly, hug, take time to visit and relax—what a concept. Soon, we all came to love her as she reached out and showed us that even we could open up and talk about our troubles. Imagine!"

"Jane was and is the true, grounded, natural change agent. She lives, models, shares, and teaches the message of love, laughter, and healing. She is a living example of the change the world needs now."

Jane was an anomaly when she married her husband, Ted, and settled into their country home in the 1960s. As most women did in that era, she took up the task of ironing the family's clothes. But she grew so bored with it that she established a routine of pouring herself a slow gin and ginger ale while watching television, just to pass the time. Despite her father's attempts at helping her to become a better housewife by donating irons, she found alternate homes for them, explaining to her father that she must have misplaced them.

"Look, I can either give up ironing or become an alcoholic," she finally said to Ted.

And so, from 1962 onward, she never ironed again.

"We showed up wrinkled."

Jane is not one to suppress her free spirit. She does not apologize for her "larger than life" nature. Her means often defy protocol or disrupt the status quo, but she takes ownership of her unconventional ways and walks tall in her truth. Through her career in education, she gained a reputation for breaking the rules in order to do what she felt was best for her students. Unless she saw it necessary, she seldom asked for permission.

"If you don't ask, then you'll never get a no," she once reasoned. It was advice she had once gotten from a friend, and she took it to heart.

This philosophy translates to every aspect of her being, including her health. In the most unorthodox ways, she has beaten the odds of injury and illness time and time again. If one tried to keep a running list of the ailments and injuries Jane has been through in her lifetime of seven decades, one would lose track. And so does she. "Just put it on the list with everything else," she once conceded to her doctor after learning she had unknowingly experienced a heart attack. Her "list" includes diagnoses for melanoma, degenerative disks in her neck and spine, an eye disorder, breast cancer, and a slew of other maladies that she can hardly recall. Over the years, she earned the nickname "The Unsinkable Molly Brown."

When she restored her torn rotator cuff through visualization and natural remedies, her surgeon praised her: "You just keep doing what you do, Jane."

It has not always been easy. When she was diagnosed with terminal breast cancer, it was one of the few moments in her life when she fell into the grip of fear. She was told that that there was only one course of action and that she would have to act fast and decisively if she was going to consider extending her life beyond a prognosis that was already too imminent. Her doctor suggested the standard course of treatment for such a diagnosis—a heavy dose of chemotherapy coupled with radiation and tamoxifen.

But Jane felt she knew her body. It was sensitive or allergic to most drugs. She is not inherently opposed to conventional medicine, yet she sees medical advances as only one star within a vast universe of healing possibilities. She did not want to trap herself into a course of action that seemed limited and impersonal. The answers are often found over, under, and beneath the crevices of an archaic "conventional-versus-alternative" dichotomy.

She contemplated all of her options, and then she went into meditations to ask her body what it truly needed to heal. When she found her answer, she called her doctor and graciously informed him that she would be refusing the prescribed course of treatment. She was so certain of her own path to healing that she walked into her surgeon's office with a polite "No, thank you" to his more radical plans, and that was the end of the discussion.

The decision was not an act of defiance, nor was it a whimsical escape from convention. It came from a deep understanding that Jane had established over years of experience. She opted to have the tumor removed, but the rest of the treatment was not consistent with what she knew to be best for her body. She grabbed a pen and crossed off the section of the surgical consent paper that mentioned her lymph nodes. They would not be coming out, nor would she be subjecting her sensitive body to chemotherapy or radiation.

Jane has engaged with the medical system where she has seen fit, yet she insists on maintaining her grasp on the reins. She keeps her sights on her unique needs and steers her health care in the direction that is right for her. In today's medical environment, this sort of autonomy is harder to achieve and rarely comes without concerted effort, sometimes even defiance. She recognizes that these health decisions we face are rarely straightforward. They are complex, and they are thorny. But they are also meant to remain in our unique hands. She stresses the importance of making one's own health decisions, even when the strong pull of convention, precedent, or protocol tugs in a certain direction.

Her resilience is a product of her will. She empowers her inner voice to guide her through illness and hardship. She repels negative thoughts and emotions, releases her fears, and focuses instead on inner peace, harmony, and laughter. She does not take ownership of diagnoses or prognoses. One often hears her say, "It is not mine to have." She visualizes herself as healthy and happy. Most importantly—every day, she sets the intention to be well, whole, and perfect in mind, body, and soul.

What she has achieved through trials and errors is a pinnacle of dominion over her mind. The power of thought is the underlying theme in every aspect of her life. Yet, perhaps the most crucial point to her story is that she does not view herself as having a unique gift. She believes that each of us has the ability, if we choose it, to direct our thoughts toward a desired end. It is a matter of gaining control of the mind, and most importantly, letting go of fear. We can all tap into the inner consciousness to heal not only the material, but also the nonphysical aspects of our being.

In truth, Jane didn't speak much of her hardships until much later in life. The personal struggles were hers to overcome, and the lessons were hers to learn. But as more of her friends encountered personal and health problems, she decided to start opening up.

"Your life will touch many," were the words of Rich Work, a spiritual teacher with whom Jane became close over several years. He was insistent that she write her story, and she sensed that it was her time to share.

There were many people throughout her life who sought her guidance, hoping to learn from her experiences. It was her interest in empowering these people through their own healing and spiritual journeys that eventually compelled her to write it all down.

The patterns of life are nonlinear—they are unpredictable, erratic, and extraordinary all at once. Most importantly, in every struggle, there is a lesson. If we choose to seek it out, it can inform our next chapter and influence outcomes that set us on a new path.

This book is arranged according to the teachings that have nurtured Jane's health and harmony. The journey begins in childhood, in the formative family sphere, and continues to follow the struggles—and their lessons—as life unfolds.

What follows is not a book of answers; it is a story of self-discovery. To ask how Jane healed herself is to inquire about her quest into the conscious self. The mental, spiritual, and physical curiosity that led her on her adventure was the same quality that at times defied convention, sparked static, and led her to persevere against the challenges. This is the story of Jane against the grain.

Introduction

Once, I was sitting on the sofa watching Eagles football with my husband, Ted, when I felt something strange happening in my heart. It was not a feeling of pain or shortness of breath. I felt as though the energy was withdrawing from my heart, like it was stopping.

I turned to my husband. "Ted, get the cuff," I said.

He went into the bedroom to get the blood pressure cuff and strapped it onto my arm. We watched the meter as nothing came up.

Then he checked my pulse in different areas. Here, again, there was nothing. He could not feel a pulse at all. When I checked, I could not feel it either.

I remained calm.

"You just keep watching the game," I said to Ted. He knew me well enough to understand that I would not want him to worry either. He sensed my calm, and he, too, remained calm.

I focused on breathing deep breaths into my body. It was an automatic reaction for me—I did not even have to think about it.

"I am fine. I am not ready to go yet. This is not my time to leave. I will be fine."

I reaffirmed myself of the inner knowing that I had. I knew I would pull out of it.

By the end of the game [I am sure the Eagles won}, I felt the energy returning to my heart and coming back to my body.

I asked Ted to get the blood pressure cuff again to check my rate. When he did, everything was back to normal; my blood pressure and heart rate were close to my regular numbers.

This event was one of two occurrences where I felt my life-force energy leave my body. In both instances, I kept calm. I did what was second nature to me: I focused on my breathing. I knew that panic would only aggravate the situation. I affirmed my inner knowing—that it was not yet my time to leave. With this affirmation, any trace of fear could be released, and instead, I could direct my thoughts and energies to my body.

1

Living Truthfully

Are they just words, or are you living proof?

My brother and I would call my mother "President of the Temperance League." To abstain from drinking was a vow she made as a young girl—a consequence of Aunt Maggie's binges that left her passed out in the bathtub. My grandfather once related the story about his sister Maggie, who once awoke from her sleep and realized that she didn't have the capacity to get herself out of the tub. She screamed and yelled until someone in the family, who was horrified by the scene of a burly woman struggling to escape the thralls of a porcelain vat, found her in the bathroom. Amid the trauma of pulling and prying at Aunt Maggie's limbs, the members of the family looked at one another and made an oath to swear off drinking for the rest of their lives. It was a promise my mother took to the grave.

It should have come as no surprise to me, then, when my mother presented me with a temperance contract when I turned twelve years old. I suppose she wanted to preserve my integrity before it could become spoiled by adolescence. The agreement stipulated that I would never, in my entire life, drink alcohol.

"With the first sip that goes past your lips," she cautioned, "you have sold your soul to the devil." In fear of this repercussion, I signed the agreement, rather uneventfully, and didn't touch liquor for the next six years of my life.

It was at church, of all places, that I reconsidered my devotion to sobriety. I had left home for college and was attending a sermon at Kutztown's Lutheran Church. I paced up to the altar and cupped my hands to accept the Holy Sacrament. Back at home, communion was grape juice, but here in Kutztown, to my surprise, it was wine. When I took my first sip of the real stuff, I felt liberated.

It was enough for me to want to embolden my brother with a similar sense of freedom. When he turned twelve, my mother dusted off the old temperance contract and set out to enforce the same regime that she had with me, seven and a half years earlier.

"Tear it up," I advised my brother, upon hearing the news of these proceedings. Years later, he would thank me for encouraging an act of such rebellion.

***

When my mother met my father for the first time, she was on a visit with her cousin, who had married my dad's sister and was living in Toronto. There, they fell in love, and he followed her back to Kensington to marry her under the condition that he would retire from smoking and drinking forever.

The women in my family all seemed to have that strong force to them—they had a risk-taking nature, a bold will, an unadorned authenticity. I inherited from my mother—who inherited from her mother—a steel spine that neither persuasion nor manipulation could bend. It was this sense of conviction and decisiveness that led me on my path the way it did my mother a generation earlier. She quit school in the eleventh grade to work as a secretary for the railroad, which lent her the special privilege of stepping on a train and going anywhere she dreamed. There is a photo of her riding a donkey down the Grand Canyon. She traveled the country by train, and she met my father that way.

She always did what she felt was right, often silently, without intention for praise. I remember finding a sweater or a blouse missing from my closet now and then, after she had determined I had not worn the item enough and consequently donated it to a neighbor. She usually never said anything about it and just left the item, anonymously, on someone's doorstep—someone, I suppose, whom she deemed needful of a new blouse.

Later in life, it was my mother's stubbornness that would prompt her to flush her arthritis pills down the toilet.

"Mom, did you take those pills that Dr. Baxt gave you?" I would ask.

"Yes, I took one and didn't like it, so I flushed the rest down the toilet," she would respond unapologetically.

Until the day she died, she would take one pill a day: an aspirin if she felt pain, or a multivitamin if she did not. Her doctor hospitalized her when she developed a kidney infection; he felt he was doing her a favor by assigning her to St. Mary's Hospital so she could be close to her parents, but he failed to realize how unwise it was to put a loyal Protestant Orangewoman into a Catholic hospital (most certainly not *my* mom). She went missing from her room almost immediately. Eventually, we found her in another patient's room, taking charge at the patient's bedside. "These nuns don't know how to take care of patients," she said. The doctor begrudgingly sent her home with recovery instructions.

I felt that my mother had psychic powers. She always seemed to know when I was sick. It did not matter where she was living; even from her retirement home in Ocean City, she would call me to ask if I was feeling ill. She was right most of the time, and even in my denial over the phone, she would sense it. She'd hang up and tell my dad to get his coat because they would be traveling to Sinking Spring to take care of their daughter. She would arrive on my doorstep, prepared to clean the house, cook dinner, and take care of me. When our first son, Roger, was born, she was so certain that he would be arriving on time, on his due date of November 29, that she scheduled the day off from work. She had been right once again.

My mother's mother, too, was emboldened with titanium conviction. She stood at a mighty four feet and eleven inches in height, but what she lacked in longitude, she made up for in bite. She was a feisty little woman. When provoked, she would often swear with the best of them under her breath. She had settled in Kensington, on Columbia

Avenue in a neighborhood called Fishtown. She immigrated to America from Belfast, the part of Northern Ireland that was struck severely by Catholic-Protestant violence in the region. Watching her parents argue over this religious divide fostered in my mother an irrevocable distrust of Catholicism for the rest of her life.

There in Fishtown, my grandmother met her husband, who had emigrated from Donegal, and they were soon married. She and my grandfather would often be seen walking on opposite sides of the street on their way to church, having just had some disagreement, usually over England. Everything would be resolved at church, and they would walk side by side to return home, her standing at four-foot-eleven and him at six-foot-one.

My grandmother loved to cook, and we would gorge on bountiful supper feasts at her table on Sundays after church. There were always two entrees: chicken and beef, or the equivalent. (Once, my grandfather refused to sit at the table until there were two entrees out). For dessert, my grandmother would make a vanilla pudding that was out of this world. She never wrote her recipes down, and if you were brave enough to ask, you would have to be quick to scribble them down as she cooked the pudding. Sundays were usually like this, spent together with my mother's parents around the dinner table, sandwiched between the morning and evening services at United Presbyterian Church. After lunch, we would listen to the radio. Even when everyone was getting televisions, we were huddled around the radio listening to the Irish hour before going back to church for the evening sermon and youth group. The only time I would step away from the Irish hour was to climb the stairs to the second radio of the household to listen to *The Shadow*, the adventures of a crime-fighting detective with psychic powers. Or I would simply find my grandfather's lap and nestle in as we listened to his hilarious stories that always seemed to tie everyone in knots.

Mainly due to my mom's strong faith, church was a big part of my upbringing. My dad was involved, too—he was on the church council—but his involvement had more to do with the sense of community than the sanctity of religion. The congregation at Norris

Square Presbyterian was primarily Scottish and Irish, and for that reason, when one walked in the door, he or she would be hugged and embraced. It was a community; we were there for each other. It was the people that made an influence in my life.

I made many cherished friends and built wonderful memories at Norris Square, save for maybe the sermons. I could not particularly remember any of them. I rarely paid attention; I went to a different place. I was a daydreamer, after all, spending so many afternoons at my desk in school, gazing out of the window and visualizing trees and flowers. I had set my intention on this vision early in my life, and it was a dream that would materialize for me years later.

Apart from the daydreaming to distract me, I was also not one for dogmatic religious principles. Part of this was attributable to an early childhood memory of being told in Sunday school that the Jews would never go to heaven because they crucified Jesus. I was seven, maybe eight years old, and the thought of my best friend, Rochelle, not getting into heaven devastated me. My mom did not understand why I was so upset when I came home crying that day. I told her that I didn't care what they said at church. I told her that I was going to get a big raincoat and tuck Rochelle under it and take her into heaven with me.

***

If he had known about it, my father would have ripped the temperance contract apart himself. While my mother belonged to the abstinence camp, my father was among the opposite. His later position as assistant superintendent of maintenance for the Pennsylvania Railroad endowed him with the coveted role of party planning. At 30th Street Station, where he was posted, there always seemed to be a reason to celebrate. There were parties to plan for holidays, retirements, birthdays, and company milestones. My father delighted in arranging the details. He was a social creature. He worked hard, but he also loved having a good time, and he wanted everyone else to have one, too.

My dad especially loved his adventures with Uncle Bob, my mother's sister's husband. Uncle Bob was a Scottish man and carried the accent that embodied his spirited nature with him until the day he died. He and my dad loved to go on adventures together that always seemed to get them into some sort of trouble. Once, they phoned me and asked if I would politely inform their wives that the two of them would be departing for a brief vacation in New England. On the trip, they rented a room in a motel that was so close to the superhighway, the beds would rumble every time a truck drove by. By morning, my dad awoke to find Uncle Bob's bed empty. He looked around and couldn't find him anywhere. He opened the door of the room and looked outside, coming upon the image of Uncle Bob, naked, doing his morning calisthenics in the parking lot.

On another of their outings, my dad noticed that a woman at the bar was giving him dirty looks. He couldn't figure out why. He later learned that Uncle Bob had been pinching the woman's rear every time she swung by him with her dance partner.

It was not until later in life that I could comprehend why my dad loved drinking—not to get drunk, but for the amusement that it facilitated in social settings. I never saw him drunk; even when others would not make it home from the party, my dad always made it home.

He just loved a good story. I suppose he found it justifiable, then, to spike the punch bowl at the company outings. I mean, heavily. Most likely with whiskey. He just wanted everyone to enjoy the holidays.

Our house on Palethorpe Street, the home in which I spent my childhood, was situated in West Kensington, a lower-middle-class neighborhood back then—not poor, but no one had much. I thought we had a lot because I never went for want. Our home was four houses away from a railroad track and an iron yard. Among other neighborhood landmarks was a paper mill, which always seemed to be on fire, and a chemical factory. There was not a blade of grass anywhere. Palethorpe Street was a dead-end street, both ways.

The old cellar's ceiling panels were the hiding place for my dad's liquor bottles—full ones on the one side and empties on the other. When his brothers and friends would come over, they would go downstairs, and that's where they would entertain themselves. Down the shore, my father and Uncle Bob would go fishing and then stop at the local watering hole called Twisty's. My father would bring Uncle Bob home to pass out on the sofa. Uncle Bob had trouble "holding his drink." My mother would sigh and say, "Oh, just look at that Uncle Bob—he is so tired," and she appeared to believe it.

I can only remember one occasion where my father drank in front of my mother. Generally, he would share a drink with his friends. He always seemed to be laughing, telling stories. He was a free spirit. In his later years, he would ride around on his big three-wheeler bicycle at the shore just to visit with people. As a milkman in Kensington, he would have a drink with the priests at the Catholic Church when he delivered their milk. But he tried his best to respect my mother's temperance by practicing discretion around her. She chose to look the other way with my father.

The one time she looked directly, they were at our shore house, and my father was holding a bottle of beer. "Put it down," she commanded, and my father proceeded to drink the entirety of its remaining swill. Out she went, slamming the door.

"She told me to put it down," he said. "She didn't say where."

The sharp contrast in their drinking philosophies was rivaled only by that of their political ideologies. My mom shook President Taft's hand as a child and became an instant Republican. My father became a Democrat when he was welcomed into America with citizenship. Upon returning from the voting booth, my mom would proudly proclaim that she had pulled the straight Republican lever, all the way down the column. My dad announced the same act with the Democratic one.

The house was never quiet; we said what we thought. There was always an interesting undercurrent in our family over these divisions. I don't know how it worked between my parents, but somehow, it did. They always left the house holding hands. There would be the occasional fight between them, but my dad had a way of charming my mom into reconciliation. He would just smile at her, beaming the twinkle in his blue eyes that everyone so admired. The friction seemed to dissolve when he would take her into the living room and sing "Let Me Call You Sweetheart."

"Let me call you Sweetheart
I'm in love with you
Let me hear you whisper
That you love me too"

My father was from Donegal, the part of the country that eventually seceded to become the Irish Free State, which in 1949 became the Republic of Ireland. Despite his country's achievement of independence, my father continued to blame all of Ireland's problems on England, just as my grandfather had. These feelings continued even in his older years, after having lived the past seven decades of his life in America.

No, his revulsion for England could not be tamed. He would be found complaining about the "witch" that kept waking him up in the middle of the night when he was in the nursing home at Cornwall Manor. The staff and his friends at the home were shocked to hear these harsh words from him, as he was otherwise a loving person. Later, it was discovered that the "witch" to which he had been referring was the night nurse, newly employed by the retirement home upon her recent emigration from England. Fortunately, the nurse graced my father with understanding and politely excused herself from his room; she replaced herself with an American substitute.

These divisions ran deep in my family, and although they ruffled feathers, they never caused war. My father had no choice but to get along, growing up in a family with eleven children. He acted on what he felt was right, for the good of his family.

Perhaps that's why, in 1923, at sixteen years old, he left his family's farm to venture across the Atlantic by boat, by himself. His parents had arranged for their eldest son, John, to make the journey to Toronto to live with his cousins, who had immigrated there a generation before. When the time came to make the journey, John could not do it. His parents, having already paid the travel fare, grew distressed over the thought of a missed opportunity. My dad, being the second oldest son of the family, quietly offered. "I'll go," he said, and he proceeded to crawl into the bowels of a ship for the journey overseas. Later, I learned the trip caused him so much nausea that he could not bring himself to step foot on a boat until years later.

My dad's parents and his siblings eventually followed his path to the United States, hoping for a better life for their family. They settled in Ithan, Pennsylvania. After my grandfather passed, my granny moved to Gulph Mills to live with my Aunt Grace and her husband, Pete. This was a house forever filled with people. Once a month, my father would take us to "Granny's" house, where all his brothers and sisters and their children would often spend Sundays. We would beg Uncle Sonny to tell stories from the war. We had seen the glorified news clips at the movies. But Uncle Sonny did not talk about it. Later, I would come to understand how horrific his experience had been while he was in the service. He had been on the front lines of World War II, serving in the Ranger brigade that went through Africa and ended up at the Battle of the Bulge. Upon hearing the name of the division in which Uncle Sonny had served, a veteran and friend of ours responded, "We were the boys; *they* were the men."

When we were together as a family, my Uncle Sonny would lead the prayer. In typical Irish humor, he would close each otherwise serious prayer with the line: "Now, may you all get to heaven thirty minutes before the devil knows you're dead."

I always liked the following Irish bit of wisdom:

> "May those who love us, love us.
> For those who don't love us, may God turn their hearts.
> And if He does not turn their hearts, may He turn their ankles,
> So we may know them by their limping."

Some of the youngest of my father's siblings ended up finishing high school in America. But my dad was a trailblazer—he was always set on being the author of his own journey (which sometimes was without Mom 's knowledge).

He would take such pride in delivering milk for Harbison's Dairy in Kensington, his first job in America. It was the prominent dairy in the neighborhood, and its factory with the giant milk bottle on its roof became an icon of the neighborhood a generation later. Dolly, my dad's horse, would pull his milk carriage around the streets of Kensington, delivering milk to the doorsteps of our friends and neighbors.

"Dolly leads the way to each stop," he would beam.

My father did not just say things. He would challenge people to act on their convictions. "Are they just words?" he would ask, "or are you living proof?" He was the living proof.

His advice to me was uncomplicated: "What people don't know won't hurt them. Care about people. Do what you can for them, but live your own truth. Don't be something that you're not just to please other people."

"Be true to yourself," were words he said to me many times.

2

Growing in Hardship

The optimist sees the rose and not its thorns;
the pessimist stares at the thorns, oblivious to the rose.
—Kahlil Gibran

I loved being the daughter of the milkman for two reasons. For one, it allowed me to skip class starting in the third grade. We "milkmaids" had the privilege of missing the class immediately preceding recess in order to prepare the milk for distribution among the students. To my delight, it was usually math.

The second reason was that it made me popular. Being the daughter of the milkman furnished one with the power to select the milkmaids whose duty was to prepare and distribute the milk and consequently miss the class prior to recess.

It is easy to see how this would be a coveted position for a third grader to find oneself in. My popularity instantly spirited me with confidence. I cherished elementary school and loved my teachers and classmates.

But it was short-lived. City school district lines redirected my newfound friends to different junior highs. I was assigned to Stetson, and the crutch of popularity was abruptly knocked out from under me.

I felt alone for the first time, trapped in a body that was quickly transforming. I grew five inches in height within seventh grade alone.

At age twelve, extending to five-foot-nine and weighing ninety pounds was not typical. My parents didn't know what to do about my growth spurt and a weight that didn't match up to it. My mom would make me milkshakes with ice cream and malt. She imagined ways to try to make me feel more comfortable by gaining weight. One can see where my love of ice cream was always front and center in my diet.

My perception of myself transformed with a force as swift as the changes in my body. Suddenly, at a stature that hovered over my peers, I felt awkward, ugly. I became acutely cognizant of my image to others, and the further I retreated into this consciousness, the greater the doubt that arose over who I was, who I appeared to be.

The new perception turned into reality. I felt awkward and became it, too. With a self-propagating momentum, I grew as vulnerable on the outside as I had been feeling on the inside. My weakened persona attracted bullying. I faced a long walk to school, and I crossed the turfs of many of my teasing classmates. I walked quickly, my head down, to get through it all. There was one boy in particular who was the ringleader of the abuse. He wouldn't leave me alone. At school, he would grab me in the hallway. He would call me names, call my family names. He made fun of the things that I believed in. I faced him in school and in church, which left me with no place to hide.

I felt my world was crumbling around me. My introversion turned into depression, and my depression paralyzed me. My friends would come to my house attempting to extract me to join them outside. Often, I wouldn't budge. I didn't want to do anything at all—eat, sleep, leave the house. I just wanted to escape from the world. I didn't care about the next day, the next week, the next year. The reality that my life had become was one I could not bear to stare in the face.

I would spend my nights reading under the covers. When the lights went out, I hid in my bed with a flashlight shining onto the words of an open book. When I opened a new book, I started reading the last chapter first. If I read it and did not like it, I would not read the rest of the book. I just had to know whether it was meant for me or not.

I began reading the works of Taylor Caldwell and her portrayals of humanity. When I began reading her work, I instantly felt a connection with her. I must have read every one of her books. Enclosed by a blanket, enlightened by a flashlight and those books, I created a separate little world for myself. I wanted to escape.

My parents worried—their outgoing daughter now having transformed radically into a silenced, recluse adolescent. Perhaps I would have turned to them for support, if it hadn't been the case that the bully's dad and mine were on the same church council. I knew how my dad would have reacted to something like this. He had a classic Irish temper. I only saw it once, but that one time made a strong impression on me.

So, I concealed it. Despite their pleading, I chose not to tell my parents the cause of my aversion to my school, my church, my neighborhood. Somehow, I knew this was my journey; I knew I needed to find my own way through it. By necessity as much as by choice, I resolved to work through the struggle on my own.

As rare an occurrence as it was in the year 1948, my parents took me to a psychologist. As in typical practice, the psychologist presented me with pictures and asked me to describe how I felt about them. I would sit in the chair and glance at the photos briefly as she presented them, and I would name them literally. "Trees. House. Church." I did not want to open the story and expose my struggle to anyone else. I wanted to stay sealed off. And I most certainly didn't want my parents to worry about me. I was protecting them as much as myself. I felt this was something I had to work through on my own.

Without knowing or questioning what had caused the changes in me, my dad found a way to open a door for me. He learned of a Quaker school in Central Philadelphia called Friends Select. What he knew was that it was a school dedicated to nurturing tolerance and understanding among youth. It was a private school and thus quite expensive, but my dad decided to work two full-time jobs in order to earn the income to be able to send me there. He left at three in the morning to come back around noon. He would sleep for a few hours, and then he worked again from four o'clock until midnight, when he would work at the railroad. The hours he put into his jobs were unimaginable, but he did, without judging or challenging. He was determined to help set me on a new path.

***

The school was in an old building. For gym class, we had to walk up a winding staircase. In the library, you could open the big window, climb out of it, go to the little store across the street for something to eat, and bring it back to the library. That's what we did.

Every day, we had our meeting where students could sit together in silence or stand up if they felt so compelled to share a thought or story. It was in this moment of reflection, seeking out our own inner light, that I first discovered a sense of inner knowing.

Once per week, we would walk to the Cherry Street Quaker Meeting House. In the front of the room were attendants—teachers, parents, others in the community. But there were no officials, no rules or restrictions in that space.

The philosophy was community; the politics were pacifist. These people would go into military service, but they would serve in non combative roles. They weren't holding guns, but they were participating through other forms of service—medical, administrative. The key, for the Quaker faith, was to be involved in helping others in any way you could—to find your inner light, to walk your truth.

First, it was my teachers who served to nourish my weakened soul. We called our teachers by their first names: Teacher Karen, Master Cliff. I had an art teacher who was six-foot-four and walked with this incredible stature. His classroom was on the top floor of the school building and had a vaulted ceiling. He arranged the easels in his class so that they were facing the center of the classroom, and he would walk through the middle of the vaulted ceiling. That image impressed upon me the concept of stature, of owning one's height. He was always telling me to stand up straight. "Look at the beauty inside, and be proud of it," he would say, his voice bold.

The warmth I felt from my classmates made me feel instantly embedded in this little community. One of my classmates was a beautiful girl, a well-known model. I knew her from the glossy ads. But in school, she would throw her arm around me, as she did with others. She even wrote in my yearbook. She would mingle with the rest of us. Here we were, lowly seventh graders, with an older student—a supermodel— taking us under her wing. It was like that at Friends Select. When there was a party in our class, everybody was invited.

It was as if we were a homogenized village. We were a small class of twenty-six kids, and classroom sizes were divided in half beyond that. Nobody cared where you came from. I knew most of the students were from well-to-do families, but they all came from different backgrounds and religions. From seventh to ninth grade, we studied the Bible thoroughly. At the end of ninth grade, we branched into other religions. Someone of the Muslim faith would come in and teach us about the Koran, and then a rabbi would come in to teach us about Judaism. This was an incredibly progressive curriculum back in the 1940s. It nurtured in me an appreciation for the lessons of the Quaker faith, whose guiding principles center on peace, tolerance for all, and the individual quest for a shining inner light. These ideals planted the seed for what would flourish into the strong belief system I continued to hold through the rest of my life.

The only practicing Quaker in our class was Clara. Like me, Clara was tall, and when I met her, I was struck by the fact that she wasn't awkward at all. Although she was quiet, she was graced with confidence. Our height created an instant partnership between us. For the first time, I realized that I was not alone in my struggle, that vulnerability was universal. It was something to embrace rather than escape. Clara was my living proof that a positive self-perception could manifest into reality.

The bonds I formed with my classmates and teachers—these breathing examples of grace—helped me to understand that we were all living a shared story. No one is alone in his or her struggles. Vulnerability is not only universal, but it is the very foundation of who we are as individuals. We can only overcome internal struggle when we learn to integrate it into our self, to practice self-love, to open ourselves to the world, to connect with others over the hardships in whatever way we can.

With each new bond I formed, I learned a lesson that helped shed another layer of self-doubt. Over these formative years, the pain began to melt away, along with the depression.

I evolved into a poised young woman, not by evading the struggle, but by integrating it into my being. It fostered a higher consciousness and impacted the course of my life. I made a point to remember what that pain felt like, to carry that understanding with me through the years. It would serve as my template for understanding students when I became a guidance counselor. I took note of the kids that were quiet or seemed alone. I spent time with them. I knew how people could fall through the cracks. I wanted them to know they were not alone, that their struggle was universal. When I came into these experiences with the goal of connecting, of getting through to these kids, I was equipped with the tools of empathy and understanding.

The depression I went through at this formative age was one of the greatest gifts of my lifetime. It set me on a path to understanding the struggles we all share. It nurtured my resilient self-confidence. It developed the foundation of my belief system, centered on peace and compassion.

It also forged my innate spiritual bond with my dad. I realized later that my dad helped awaken me to an open way of looking at everything. His Irish influence of approaching life with humor and light-heartedness, of accepting everyone, and of following the heart above all else would become my mantra as I navigated through life's issues.

Out of the worst times, there is a gift.
One just needs to believe, have patience, and be open to it.

3

Discovering the Path

Each one of us has a unique life's journey.
How much of it we come to understand and achieve is up to us.

"Why, Jane, don't you just follow the *rules*?"

My high school boyfriend looked back from his seat in front of me, frustrated. He had noticed my tests being returned with Fs, and he felt compelled to assist me in understanding how algebra worked. He was getting straight As, and he tried handing his exams back to me, pointing to the neatly organized steps numbered one through four.

My answers had been correct. It was my process that was falling short. It's not that I didn't understand the rules; it's that I didn't care for them.

"If I'm getting the right answers, why do I have to do the problems in a certain way?" I would ask the teacher.

He was a teacher whom my best friend Janet thought was great, at the time. I felt he represented everything I opposed.

For him, it had to be linear; it had to follow his pattern. My way of thinking looped in circles and scribbles, not boxes and lines. I didn't want to be following someone else's rules if I didn't see a purpose to them. I was arriving at the answers in my own way, and I felt that was sufficient.

I felt I wasn't the one who had to adjust—it was the teacher that needed some loosening up. If my previous experience at Friends Select had endowed me with confidence, I was certainly not afraid to show it. For the first marking period, I continued to place my answers in a circle when the requirement was to mark them in the box.

And for the entirety of the first marking period, the teacher refused to grade my tests and my homework. Since neither of us would budge, *F* marked the spot.

My resistance could not sustain itself into the second marking period. I knew I needed to pass the class because I had set my sights on college. I wanted to become a guidance counselor. I couldn't be failing math.

The teacher worked out an arrangement with me. He recommended that I come into his class after school to work on the assignments. If I committed to staying after school with him and working out the problems in the order in which he had established for his students, he would allow me to redeem my grade.

I reluctantly submitted. In demonstration of my defiance, I would take the seat directly in front of him so that we would be seated face to face. When I walked into his quiet classroom, I would take my stack of books and drop them onto my desk, causing a loud "thud." It was my way of telling him I was there without saying anything.

It continued like this, every week, after school, as I plopped my books onto the desk and completed the homework assignments as he asked, in the way that he demanded. In time, he allowed me to redeem myself with a B average for the school year (although I still refused to acknowledge any wrongdoing on my part).

Meanwhile, Janet and I had forged an instant bond when we met at Frankford High. Since I was coming from a private junior high, I was able to go to any high school of my choosing. I decided on Frankford High, not only because it was one of the best high schools in Philadelphia back in the early fifties, but also because I pictured it taking me away from Kensington and setting me in a place surrounded by grass.

I remember walking into my homeroom on the first day of school, knowing not a soul, but feeling comfortable in my skin. In homeroom, I met a girl who would become my lifelong friend, Janet. It was a large school at the time—filled with about three thousand students—and I think Janet took pity on me because I knew no one. She had come from a popular junior high where many students matriculated to Frankford. She invited me to join her sorority (which existed in high schools back then). I joined, but I still mingled with everyone.

As my audacious nature continued to flourish, so did my height. I was so tall that my mom made most of my clothes. I had a few skirts and a few blouses, and that was it. My limited wardrobe was narrowed even further if my mother thought I wasn't wearing something often enough. She would just give it away. Teenage years often involved girls and how they looked, but I never cared much. Some of my friends encouraged me to wear makeup, but it just didn't feel like me. I was not so concerned about my image to others. When other girls would talk about their clothing, I remember thinking to myself, *I am glad I am me.*

I was forever laughing, tripping, doing my own thing. In high school, a friend of mine gave me the nickname Calamity Jane, a moniker that, unbeknownst to me at the time, would be perfectly suited for my life's tumultuously wild—and most certainly *non*linear—pattern. It stuck.

***

The accident happened when I was in Ocean City, New Jersey, on vacation with my family. Since I was the age of twelve and well into my college years, my family spent summers in Ocean City. I would get jobs waiting tables or scooping ice cream at the Top of the Wave. I was known for giving huge dips of ice cream. People took photos of my ice cream dips, just so they could show Mr. Allen, the owner, how big I could make them. I remember drawing laughter from one couple when they ordered an ice cream soda, and instead of using seltzer, I used water. The guy was in hysterics. In his laughter, he gave me a quarter as my tip. When most tips were a dime and our hourly wage was maybe thirty cents an hour, a quarter was a sizable tip!

My friend Barbara had the "Barbara Banana" car, and we would all put in a quarter for gas (back when gas was a quarter a gallon). One time, we ran out of gas and had to push the car to the gas station. We would do anything for gas money then, just so we could ride around Ocean City. In our college years, we would spend summers there. We had so little money that we would comb the beach collecting bottles to cash them in for two cents each. We traveled between whichever one of our parents' houses had a better stock of food in it, Barb's or mine. Our parents brought food with them when they came down on weekends, and during the week, we scavenged what was left. When our summer job started, we stashed milkshakes in the garbage out back, and when our shift ended, we snuck around to grab them and take them home.

We had not a care in the world. We had big beach parties with kids playing ukuleles around the bonfire. Before we had our driver's licenses, we'd just stick our thumbs up and hitch a ride to get to the boardwalk. That was generally our way of getting around. We hung out at Ma's Cabin, a small restaurant at the end of the island that had a soda fountain and a jukebox. We all danced together. Nobody really went with anybody; it was just one friendly crowd of kids. It was a simpler time.

By senior year, most everybody was smoking cigarettes except for me. I had a fear of fire and was too afraid to light a match.

I once turned to Barbara to ask for hers. "Just lend me yours and I'll puff on it," I said. When she gave it to me, I started chewing the end instead of puffing it.

Barbara swiped it back from me immediately. "Forget it," she said as she rolled her eyes.

The night of the accident, my friends and I were having a pajama party, and we were all wearing pajama tops with shorts and high heels. I remember that my parents were out of town because my grandfather was sick. My parents left for Philadelphia to be with him, and I was in the house by myself. With my parents' permission, I decided to have a pajama party, and so I got all of my girlfriends together. We all met at the Top of the Wave in our pajama tops and shorts and high heels. I am certain we looked ridiculous. We all went into the eatery and bought raw hamburger patties. We were going to take them back to my house to have a cookout.

We couldn't resist when the guys came with their car; we quickly abandoned our original plan to walk back to my house. Some of us jumped into the car, while some of us simply found a place to step onto it and hang on. I was standing on the running board, with the bag of raw hamburger in one hand and holding onto the center piece of the car with the other hand, which also held my shoes. Suddenly, we turned a corner, and my friend Rita cried out that she was falling. I went to grab her with the hand I had been using to hang onto the car, and when I reached for her, I flew off and landed with my head on a rock.

It took only a few moments for the ambulance to arrive. When they put me on the gurney and set route for the hospital, tears started pouring down my cheeks.

"I'm not crying," I insisted as I wiped them away, "I'm just allergic … I have an allergy … that's what's causing the tears."

I didn't want to admit I felt any pain. "I just have to get my things and go home so I can go to work tomorrow," I said. "I have to go get my uniform."

The doctors indicated that I had fractured my skull, and they housed me in the maternity ward at Shore Memorial Hospital for the next two nights because they had nowhere else to put me. They administered a spinal tap every day to check if the blood had left my spinal fluid. And every day of the two weeks I spent in the hospital, I had my friends sneak in hot fudge sundaes and milkshakes. Ice cream was on my personally approved medicine list; it was just never on the list that doctors outlined for me, which included staying off of the beach.

Now, who, at sixteen, could do that while being a few blocks away from the beach?

"Someday," my doctors warned, "you'll be sorry for not listening to our instructions."

It was not until years later that I learned what those warnings meant.

The local newspaper ran a front-page article about us. It was entitled: "South-End Kids Run Wild."

***

September arrived, and I went back to the classrooms of Frankford High, where I ran into a boy I had known in grammar school. His name was Billy. In grammar school, I remember the principal coming into our class. He asked everyone to stand up and clap for Billy because Billy had the highest IQ in the school.

"IQ measures what you can do," said the principal. "Billy's IQ means he can do anything."

Billy and I had attended separate junior highs, and then we both ended up at Frankford for high school. When I saw him there, we started talking. He told me something that would serve as a catalyst for my life's career choice.

He said to me, "Jane, I think I am going to quit school."

He explained how, when his brothers and sisters were sick, he had to stay home and take care of them so his mom did not have to miss work. His dad wasn't in the picture, so Billy was going to drop out to stay home with his siblings. He also held a full-time job at night to help pay the bills. At the time, I wasn't sure what guidance counselors did, but I thought this was something they advised on, so I suggested to Billy that he see a guidance counselor.

He took my advice and sought guidance with the school's counselor. After the meeting, he came and found me. He told me that the counselor advised him to quit school so he could help take care of his siblings. I was shocked by the advice he had received. Was Billy not meant to continue learning? Was his life's purpose merely to remain home to provide care to his siblings? I felt saddened by this bleak prospect for Billy's future.

The reason for my adolescent struggle was starting to manifest in clear form. I realized that, just as my community in junior high had guided me to work through hardship by finding my inner light, this encounter with Billy would help me in my chosen vocation. I felt compelled to share what I had learned and help others. I had never forgotten what it felt like to struggle with pain, to grapple with questions over identity and self. My adolescent depression was not just an obstacle for me to overcome; it was also the gift that I was meant to share. I later learned the importance of this gift.

Without knowing anything about a counselor's role, other than a notion that they had to care about their students, I knew I was meant to be one.

The only problem was that my dad didn't believe in girls going to college. Even though he worked two full-time jobs to send me to Friends Select, his beliefs carried over from his old-world upbringing. He generally questioned the value of higher education, and especially so for girls. In his mind, he had attended "the college of life." He did not make it past grammar school, but he was the smartest man I knew. I remember how he would help my brother with his homework, without having ever taken the class himself.

I was surprised, then, when he sat me down one day to discuss the prospect of attending college.

"Ok," he said. "I will allow you to go to college on the condition that you get an A average your senior year."

That was all I needed to hear to turn my dreams into reality. With determination, I dedicated myself to my schoolwork. I made sure to take the classes I loved, since it was the senior year's grade point average that counted. I achieved an A average.

When I turned down the scholarship to go to Temple, my guidance counselor was alarmed. She thought I was making a mistake, but I longed to leave the city behind. I wished to stay true to my childhood visualization of being surrounded by grass and trees.

Begrudgingly, the counselor handed me a pile of college catalogs and told me to find what I wanted from the list. I remember spreading out the catalogs all over the floor in her office as I started thumbing through them. Any students that came in had to step over me to get to her desk. I exuded a tinge of passive rebellion, I suppose.

***

Kutztown was the only state teachers' college offering undergraduate degrees in counseling at the time, so I knew it was the right place for me. I worked many jobs so that I could pay for my first year there. I wanted to prove to my father that college was a worthwhile endeavor, even for girls. After the first year of doing well at school, my father agreed to pay for the remainder of my college tuition.

My mother continued to tend to my wardrobe, perhaps because she was concerned that I was not. Once, she met me at 30th Street Station so I could try on a dress that she had made me for a visit with my friend at Rensselaer Polytech Institute in Troy, New York. It was an aqua-blue gown with pink lining, and I remember laughing in the bathroom stall at 30th Street Station after a failed attempt to zip it up because my mother had sewn the zipper into the wrong side. Nonetheless, I brought it with me to Rensselaer, showing it off proudly. All of the girls there were visiting from these prestigious colleges. When they asked and I told them I went to Kutztown State Teachers' College, it was both the beginning and the end of the conversation.

It was in college that I met my husband, Ted. I liked him from the moment I met him. When our group of friends organized a caving trip together, I made sure that Ted was invited. We all entered the cave, and as soon as we came out of it, I knew I was meant to marry him. He didn't know it, but I did.

On our first date, I spilled my milkshake all over him, the car, and myself. I thought, *I better find a way to ditch my Calamity Jane nickname fast if I am going to make a good impression on my husband-to-be.*

I graduated from Kutztown with a double major in social studies and guidance and a minor in English. I started my education career in both fields at Brandywine High School in 1958. When I went in for the interview with the superintendent at Brandywine, I told him I didn't feel qualified to be the full-time guidance counselor. I always said what I felt, even at the risk of compromising my position.

Despite my naive admission, I got the job. Perhaps the superintendent felt I was the only one foolish enough to take on the task-load for a humble $3,800 a year. I was glad to accept it, and I served as the sole full-time guidance counselor for grades seven through twelve—in fact, I was the only guidance counselor for the district.

When tasked with the goal of designing an honors society for the school, I knew I did not want the top kids separated from the rest—I wanted them helping their classmates. So, I designed the program so that each honor society student was required to give up a certain amount of time to mentor students in need of help. I took a page from the program at Frankford High, where the honors society leader encouraged this same exchange.

I learned a great lesson while developing a testing program for the elementary school students. I had only worked with teenage students before. There were guidelines available, so establishing the test itself was not difficult. *Administering* it to the little ones—that was a different story. Before testing, we went through sample questions together. I always tried to make sure the students had a good understanding of how the questions were set up. One of the samples involved a cat. When I asked the students what questions they had regarding the sample, bedlam prevailed. They were all so excited to tell me about not only their own cats, but also about other feline friends they knew of. I struggled to get them focused on the test again. I remember laughing afterward when I realized I had lost control of these first-graders. I learned a humbling lesson that day about the uninhibited nature of children.

Midway through the school year, the principal sat me down and told me he couldn't believe I had been so naive in front of the superintendent about my ability to serve as a full-time counselor. It was only my first year, and yet I managed to set up the new testing program for the school district; I taught fifteen hours of Pennsylvania history each week; I taught guidance classes; I managed a study hall and a homeroom; I set up an honors society; and I taught a life-adjustment course to seniors. I often wondered how we all did what we did back then.

I loved my years at Brandywine. Apart from the wonderful students, the tight-knit group of faculty members made the job fun and fulfilling. Mr. Moll would bring Applejack brandy to the teachers' picnic sessions for all the new and unsuspecting teachers. One of the beloved teachers,

Mrs. W., would make up brandy Alexanders in her thermos bottle for the in-service days. There was a great camaraderie among us; it was a faculty who greatly cared about each other and our students—even at a $3,800 salary. None of us were paid very much at the start. The physical education teacher, Bob, was not even paid for the three sports he coached when he started. He had to make sure the fields were mowed and lined with the help of his players, and he also had the responsibility of being the athletic director, with no compensation for his first several years. The faculty was driven by its passion for the students, surely not by their salaries.

I moved to a new school and became the counselor at Conrad Weiser Junior and Senior High School. This was an easy transition for me. Although I was still the only counselor and had guidance classes, the counselor before me, Roe Koste, had set up an excellent program. I also inherited the school's student council, which, due to the enthusiasm of its members, I enjoyed greatly.

Dr. Shankweiler, the superintendent, had a keen eye for what was needed in his district, and he was greatly admired by his staff. Again, I was fortunate to find myself in a school where the faculty and students held close bonds. My memories of the staff and students were and still are special to me.

I was only there for a year when I became pregnant with our oldest son, Roger. After he was born, I went back to college to finish my master's degree in counseling at Temple University, which had a great program in cooperation with local colleges. Then, in September of 1963, I ended up at Governor Mifflin High School. After a few years, I took time off to try to have a second child, which I did, with the birth of our second son, Robb.

While I was home with Robb, the superintendent at Mifflin convinced me to return to school for a designated number of hours per week to help pregnant teens. The industry standard back then was to force these girls to leave school upon becoming pregnant. It always troubled me immensely that girls had to quit school as soon as anyone found out about their pregnancy. Girls would disguise themselves in loose clothing and conceal their truth in fear of being kicked out. I never hesitated to let my feelings be known about this practice.

I agreed to work with the pregnant teens; I knew graduation would be important for them. Since I was able to spend time with them each week, I was able to focus my energy on their needs. I taught the girls about childcare, parenting skills, where to find maternity clothing, and baby food. As I had accreditation in social studies and English, I also taught them both of these regular courses so that they could earn credit toward graduation.

After two years of working with these young girls, the school asked if I would return as a guidance counselor. This was a hard decision for me, as it meant being away from Robb, who was three at the time. When the school offered me the option of working on a part-time basis, I accepted.

From the start of my career at Brandywine to the end at Governor Mifflin, I always tried to tailor student programs and clubs to the unique group I was working with, depending on the student's skill levels as well as their personalities and interests. My biggest goal was to ensure these programs were worthwhile. I wanted the students to truly get something out of them. I would set an outline and oversee it, but I would let the students design and implement the programs.

In this second tenure as a counselor at Mifflin in the late '70s, I decided to gear my energies toward youth empowerment with the creation of a short class I called Communication Skills. Even though it was a great group of students, there were some who felt isolated, and I wanted them to experience a different scenario. As per my philosophy, I wanted to ensure that any program would be worthwhile.

"Anything that gets said in this classroom stays in this classroom." I would make this announcement at the beginning of the Communication Skills class. (This was before Las Vegas took over the slogan, of course).

One time, the assistant superintendent asked if he could come to the class to observe. By now, he knew I did many things without asking for permission. He never seemed to mind. I thought about it for a moment. I wanted to preserve the open and honest nature of the class that the students had come to embrace. I agreed to allow him to attend on the condition that he would be known by his first name, Stanley, once he stepped into the class, and that he would have to abide by the rules the class had set forth.

And I reminded him of our golden rule: "What is said here stays here."

I had attended one of Jack Canfield's workshops and fell in love with his philosophies on youth empowerment. *101 Ways to Develop Student Self-Esteem and Responsibility* was one of the books that served as a guide for the class. Students played icebreaking games, discussed strengths, and acknowledged weaknesses. We were blindfolded and did trust walks. We role-played. It was a diverse group of students, and soon, the group began to meld. I made a point to invite a mixture of students with different personality types, including academic-oriented students as well as those lacking in self-confidence or who did not like school. I wanted the kids to learn from each other and accept one another rather than be led by their prejudices. There were a couple of students who stood out to me as needing a paradigm shift. I hoped to change their viewpoints.

Soon, this vision was realized. I would see the students in the hallway laughing or hugging, and some of these were kids who did not know or accept each other before this. I encouraged them to learn from one another, to keep an open mind. It was a matter of getting a diverse group of kids together and then taking them out of their normal world for a period each week. They started appreciating their differences and similarities. I smiled at the living proof that it *is* possible for students to understand how similar they are, how they are all writing a shared story.

Another program that I was involved in was the Berks Teen Institute, or BTI. It was a club established in many Berks County high schools dedicated to the idea of promoting positive self-image and staying drug-free. The great aspect of the club was that it was focused on positive outreach between students. I saw myself only as a group facilitator. I felt this promoted empowerment among the teenagers and helped develop relationships that adults could not have duplicated.

A former student, Kristen, shared her thoughts with me on being a part of BTI as a student: "I thought of BTI as a support group for kids who wanted to do the right thing. It was a club that did not demand much in one way—little time, talent, and practice—but in other ways, demanded quite a lot. Each year, when I signed up for the program, I thought about the commitment to stay drug- and alcohol-free. I meant what I committed to. I felt as though signing up for BTI was taking any further decision-making about drinking off the table for another year of my high school life. The spirit of BTI was about being involved in things together—older kids paired up with younger ones; students who struggled were supported by students who had some kind of strength to give at the time. It was a club for people who cared, and that was something that really spoke to me in those early days of building an identity as a teenager."

In my career, I would give talks on depression and stress management to students and faculty alike. My experience with depression as an adolescent helped me to better understand and relate to a range of people. I learned these lessons the hard way, and the experience came to infuse my teaching philosophy. In my eyes, every new student came to me with a clean slate. Underneath the surface, we all have the same need to be understood and accepted.

Over the years, I built close bonds with faculty and students, and I continued many of these friendships well past my retirement. I suppose I cracked the mold when it came to protocols and precedents. I did what I felt was needed to get through to my students. When my teaching colleagues came to me worried about a good student whose grades were slipping suddenly, I asked him to see me. He didn't want to talk in my office. So, without asking permission, I took him out for a walk in the country because I knew he enjoyed being outdoors and thought it might make him feel more comfortable. We went to a quiet area that he enjoyed and walked until he was ready to talk. He finally opened up. We were able to resolve the problem, and he began earning good grades again. I often did things like this—breaking from convention, often breaking the rules—to do what I felt in my own heart was right.

Unless they were focused and direct, I often felt meetings were overrated. I tended to find ways to get out of them, especially when they interfered with my time in my office with students.

I probably came close to compromising my career at various times. I said what I felt. I felt it was important to be direct, to speak my mind. If an issue was related to someone else, I would directly address that person. I rarely had a problem standing up for what I believed in or breaking the rules to stay true to this philosophy. I often opted *not* to ask for permission. As a dear friend once advised me: "If you don't ask, then you'll never get a no."

"Jane had an enormous impact on the students and was admired by many on the faculty because of the positive force of her personality. She became an expert on depression and stress and was fearless in taking on difficult personal and family problems. I have known few people in my career in education who were such strong advocates for students. At times, she irritated some administrators because of the lengths to which she would go to help kids who were acting out. One administrator made the criticism that Jane believed there was good in everyone.

It was her faith and openness with students that empowered many of them to take responsibility for their own lives. They were able to begin to make better decisions, which helped their personal growth and healing."

—Tom Wenrich
Friend and Colleague

4

Against the Grain

*Remember that the airplane takes off
against the wind, not with it.*
—Henry Ford

I found myself in the liquor store among the whiskey bottles looking for a whole-grain alcohol for a cleanse.

"One hundred ninety proof," I replied to the cashier when he asked what I was looking for.

He winced at my response, looking perplexed.

"What on earth do you want to do with that?" he challenged.

"It's for a homeopathic treatment," I replied innocently.

"Hmm," he said with a discerning look as he reached under the counter for the bottle, "you sure are the only one."

***

I have rarely been afraid of breaking the rules in life, and in fact, I have often found little rewards on the "other side" of protocol.

Once, my friends Ellen, Mary, and I were at a Hay House event at the Academy of Music in Philadelphia to hear Dr. Wayne Dyer give a lecture. When we entered the building, we looked at our tickets to locate our seats. Although our section was straight ahead on the first floor, I decided we should go to the right.

My friends stopped me. "Jane, we are supposed to go *this* way."

"Oh, it's fine," I told them. "Let's see if we can't get those box seats."

I grabbed my friends and brought them down the hallway to the right, where we ended up on a beautiful box balcony overlooking the stage. We had hit the jackpot. We took a moment to bask in our glory, as I took my shoes off and Ellen started stretching out in yoga poses on the floor. All this space! And the view! We decided we would stay.

Dr. Dyer started the event, and his lecture was inspiring, as it always is. At the event's closing, a singer entered the stage to sing "Wind Beneath My Wings," one of my favorite songs, which she dedicated to Dr. Dyer. A few minutes into the song, who should show up at our box but Dr. Dyer himself. Ellen got up off of the floor, and I threw my shoes back on. But he seemed not to notice the spectacle we were making of ourselves. Instead, he entered the space and stood next to us. We all put our arms around each other and started swaying to the song together. Dr. Dyer had always been a personal hero of mine, and when this moment struck, I realized it was all meant to be; we had found ourselves in the right place at the right time, simply by following my whims.

It is this very sort of unconventional thinking that led me on the healing path I still walk today. I was prompted to take a "left turn" when conventional medicine failed to heal me time and time again. My sensitive body prompted me to find an alternative path, and I was fortunate to find a trusted natural doctor and advisor who helped light the way. Yet, even when I started down the alternative path, I never stopped adapting and adjusting according to my own needs and desires; I often dismissed the protocols to pursue the course of action I felt was right for me.

***

As my career in education was blossoming, my role as a lifelong student was tested once again. In those early years in my career, I was faced with a series of health difficulties that would serve as the catalyst for a major evolution in my wellness paradigm.

My headaches began my first year of teaching. They were violent, undoubtedly a residual effect of my fractured skull years before. I went to a doctor of osteopathic medicine for adjustments, but the headaches had a way of coming back. In addition to the headaches, I got double ear infections and developed an allergy to antibiotics in the same year. For the next ten years, I would get pneumonia two times annually. Every antibiotic my doctor prescribed brought about another allergic reaction.

I remember a time when, after having pneumonia twice a year for ten years, I landed in the hospital once again, unable to breathe. My doctor told me that if it happened one more time, he was sending me down South with a bottle of whiskey. He knew milkshakes were my preferred drink.

There I stood, helpless, allergic to most antibiotics and without a plan for tackling the maladies being thrown my way. Somehow, I knew to stay open. I sensed that whatever or whomever I would need in life would come to me.

And then one day in 1985, I received a phone call from my friend Marilyn.

"I found someone with gifts similar to Edgar Cayce's," she said excitedly.

Edgar Cayce was a healer, and I had been reading a lot about him in those years. He was someone who had the ability to go into a trance and recommend a natural treatment for someone simply upon hearing his or her name. I grew fascinated by this concept, these connections between people and the energies surrounding us. *The Sleeping Prophet*, a book written by Jess Stern about Edgar Cayce's regressions into past lives, was my initiation to the world of alternative healing. I connected with the stories and the meaning, and I was hooked.

So when my friend called me to tell me she had found the "Mrs. Edgar Cayce," I was intrigued. I did not know at the time that this woman, Dr. Carrie, would become one of the greatest gifts of my life. I called her to make an appointment. At the time, I had a rash of blisters that were appearing around my upper thighs. I tried various prescriptions and remedies for months to get rid of them, with no success. When I mentioned them to her, she suggested the most unusual remedy: buttermilk.

I went to the store to buy a quart of buttermilk, and then I followed her instructions to slather it around my thighs where the rash was appearing. The very next day, it had cleared from my skin.

I wanted to connect my father with her. He was suffering from the symptoms of Parkinson's, and he was reacting negatively to the drugs his doctors were prescribing. His body, like mine, was sensitive to many types of drugs. When Dr. Carrie met him, she gave him a series of topical remedies. Gradually, they began to take hold. His blood pressure went back to normal. Most importantly, he did not shake again.

I was sold. I began sharing my health history with Dr. Carrie. I told her about my sensitivities to drugs, about my history of pneumonia, about my headaches. She was able to identify reasons for many of these health problems. She held degrees in physics and metaphysics. She worked with people who were interested in finding answers through alternative methods.

Dr. Carrie deemed that I had an extremely toxic body, possibly from growing up between a chemical factory and an iron yard. She had me taking baths in silver polish to pull out metals. It seemed wild to me, but the natural treatments she recommended were taking hold. As new ailments arose, I followed her prescriptions, taking baths and mixing natural concoctions.

Suddenly, I was reliving the wisdom of my grandparents, who used baking soda to reduce acid in the body. I discovered the wonder drug of mustard. I was taking mustard packets from restaurants and eateries, storing them in my pocketbook, using them for every possible ailment to withdraw debris. I was forever turning my ankle, and I always put the mustard pack between my sock and my ankle to reduce swelling and bruising. When I felt chilled, I sipped Tia Maria, and for a cough, there was peach schnapps. Special baths relieved my headaches. Pear nectar and vitamins D and C replaced my flu shots. I gargled coffee [while saying vowel sounds] if I felt a virus coming on. I drank red grape juice for severe sore throats.

My headaches ceased. My pneumonia stopped coming back. Finally, something worked that my body could accept.

"We underestimate our body's ability to self-heal," reasoned Dr. Carrie.

***

When I was in my thirties, I went to see a neurosurgeon, Dr. H. J., in Reading. He was a very serious person, and I sensed there was no fooling around with him. One plus one equaled two, and you didn't talk to him about anything else. Nonetheless, my family doctor had referred me to him, as he was the best in his field.

When I went to see Dr. H. J., I couldn't move my neck or my arm. The testing showed a degenerating disc of the neck. Dr. H. J. recommended surgery on the disc and explained that I would be in intensive care for twenty-four hours after the operation.

"Oh, no, I'm not," I assured. "My parents are coming here to see me. I must be sitting up in a chair and smiling when they come."

My will prevailed. Sure as anything, I was sitting up in the chair next to my hospital bed the day following the surgery when my parents came to see me. The neurologist came to check on me, and he asked me to lift my left arm and swing it. I couldn't, but I was stubborn enough to prove that I could, so I reached for my right arm to prop up the left one. On the way, I smacked the surgeon square in the face, knocking his glasses off.

I erupted in laughter. I mean, I was in complete hysterics—the doctor, not so. He left the room, scoffing that I could expect to remain hospitalized for ten days as I recovered.

Later, the nurse asked the neurologist what he thought of me, to which he remarked, "That woman has the longest arms in the world."

A few days later, I was getting bored of being in a hospital bed. I thought it would be fun to make a bubble bath, so I added Prilosec to my bathwater. My nurse caught me when I accidentally switched on the call button, mistaking it for the bathroom light. The nurse gained a few gray hairs from me that week, to say the least.

Despite the pain we were in, my hospital roommate and I decided to roam the neurosurgery wing to cheer up the other patients. My doctor seemed so distant, and people were in there for brain tumors and other dire conditions. We wanted to brighten the place up, so we would visit with patients and crack jokes. We tried to have a good time while concealing our pain.

I was dismissed from the hospital six days early and back at school in a few weeks, defying my doctor's predictions for recovery. He had notified the school that I would be missing the rest of the school year, but I think he was happy to see me leave.

The next time I saw my neurosurgeon was for a follow up visit a few weeks later. Jokingly, he asked me to step to the far side of the room before attempting to lift and swing my arms. He was laughing. However, he got very serious and concerned when he again stressed what my future held due to the condition of the discs in my neck and back. According to him, X-rays do not lie. He felt I would be seeing a lot of him, as his prediction was that my mobility would be constrained.

I thought to myself. *Even the hardest person has emotions.* I later came to realize that perhaps the reason why he seemed cold to many was because he had to be in control of his emotions as he worked with such big life-and-death decisions. I later discovered that this same doctor was so distraught by the death of a child patient that he had showed up at the child's family's front door late at night to express his grief. Sometimes, we don't know people's true capacity for connection. We don't see it on the surface, but it is there, even when we don't expect it.

I remember vividly my father's advice: Don't let someone else determine things for you. Think for yourself. Sometimes that means breaking the rules to do what is best for somebody, including you.

I often found myself in trouble with doctors as I skipped out on an appointment or crossed out a section of the surgical consent paper with a polite "No, thank you." Sometimes, I break the rules unintentionally. Other times, it is a conscious act of rebellion. When I enter a doctor's office, I tend to cause one of two reactions: I'm either making that doctor laugh or causing him or her to pull his or her hair out. My intention is not to defy authority, but rather to put myself first. Dr. Newman, my earlier doctor, once told me that I know "the secret." He elaborated that I know my body and I honor it. What I feel my body needs, I ask for.

Case studies show that those who question authority in hospitals are actually more likely to recover from cancer than those who take everything at face value. According to psychological research on cancer patients by Dr. Bernie S. Siegel, outlined in his book, *Love, Medicine and Other Miracles*, the so-called "problem patient" is also the rapid healer, the long-term survivor, and the one with the active immune system.

"When a nurse tells me that a patient is being uncooperative, refusing to get undressed and put on the standard hospital gown, or asking all sorts of questions before submitting to a test, I say, 'Fine. He'll live longer,'" explains Dr. Siegel in his book.

He encourages people to behave as individuals when they enter a hospital by following a list of suggestions he calls "Good Patient, Bad Patient," which includes:

1. Take room decorations of personal and inspirational nature. Make sure your room has a view of the sky and outside world.
2. Question authority—tests, etc. Speak up for yourself, both before and during tests.
3. Make your doctor aware of your unique needs and desires. Offer to share books, tapes, and conversation.
4. Tell the surgeon to speak to you during surgery, honestly but hopefully, and also to repeat positive messages but absolutely avoid negative ones.
5. Speak to your own body, particularly the night before surgery, suggesting that the blood leave the area of surgery and that you'll heal rapidly.
6. Get moving as soon as possible after surgery.

Indeed, there is a certain type of patient who thrives in medical settings. This individual is bold, perhaps audacious. She is confident in what she wants and needs, and she dares to ask for it specifically. Sometimes, perhaps often, she questions decisions. She may defy authority. She may stir up trouble. She is not only digging out the root of the problem. She is building her own shovel.

***

I do not limit my rule-breaking to the conventional medical arena—I do plenty of unorthodox things within the world of alternative medicine, too. Despite my personal alignment with most of the homeopathic and natural practices, I still find the need to adapt some of them to my own needs. I never stop adjusting and re-aligning these healing methods to my inner knowing, and that has been the key to my success in the world of alternative healing. These remedies do not act alone; they must be reinforced by our intentions.

Take the example of peanut butter. I cannot stand it. So when Dr. Carrie recommended a half-cup of peanut butter as a remedy, I objected. "There's no way I can do that," I told her. I thought about alternatives, and then I went back to her.

"How about Reese's Peanut Butter Cups instead?" I asked Dr. Carrie. I knew I could get the peanut butter down, so long as it was covered in chocolate.

"I don't think so," she said.

But on my encouragement, she looked into it.

When she came back to me, she sighed in concession. "I don't believe this, Jane. But I am receiving information that the peanut butter cups will work."

The same went for ice cream. It would be hard to give it up, even though it is not on Dr. Carrie's "approved foods" list.

"I will make sure it is from happy cows!" I reassured her.

I have shared some of these general remedies with others to help them through hardship, as I have shared my positive thinking on their behalf. When my parents were in the retirement center at Cornwall Manor, they had a daily regimen to help with aches and pains. They would get witch hazel rubbed around their faces and necks to get the gases out in the morning and at night, a rub-down of baking soda mixed with water to help pull acid out of the body. Drinking pear nectar was their flu shot, and it worked.

We were fortunate to have such a wonderful and open doctor there, who approved of all of our alternative medicine regimens. He finally came around to asking me, "Jane, what can I do for your parents?" He did not feel he was doing enough because they were so great at taking their health and wellness into their own hands with these remedies.

"Hug them," I told the doctor. "Hug them, and give them back rubs." And he did. In fact, I saw him giving a shoulder rub to a person in a wheelchair, and I felt great joy in seeing a conventional doctor who was so open to alternative forms of healing and the power of touch.

I often share what works with family, friends, colleagues, students—whomever may be interested in healing themselves in a more natural way.

When I was working as a counselor, one of my students fell and hurt his shoulder while practicing pole vaulting for the state championship. He was concerned that he wouldn't heal in time for the championship. I saw the look of worry on his face. I asked him, "Are you open to trying some unusual healing techniques?"

He said, eagerly, "Yes; I will try anything."

I called his mother and asked her the same question. I told her that if he was open to trying out the alternative methods, I would call Dr Carrie for suggestions, so long as I had her permission. "Yes, anything," she said.

States were a couple of days away. I called Dr. Carrie. She saw a lot of acid in this boy's body. She recommended that we make a paste out of baking soda and water and rub the paste on his shoulder. She also recommended he eat a can of cream of potato soup mixed with a can of water. (This soup helps to pull acid out of out the body and is also great for an upset stomach). There were remedies to be started as soon as possible and others to be done later at home with his mother.

I was anxious to get the healing process moving, and I did not waste a minute. On my lunch break, I rushed to the grocery store for the soup and baking soda. I went back to the school and straight to the home economics suite for a pan to mix the baking soda with water. I used the faculty microwave to heat up the cream of potato soup mixed with water. During his free period, I had the student in my office, eating soup and sitting with a slather of baking-soda paste on his shoulder. I instructed him to repeat the same method at home as often as possible over the next couple of days, in addition to other treatments Dr. Carrie had recommended. Sure enough, he healed enough to make it to states.

Looking back, I wonder what people would have thought if they had seen a student with a gooey, white paste all over his shoulder sitting in the guidance office, eating cream of potato soup. At the time, I did not think much about others' perceptions or judgments; it was not the first time I strayed from the beaten path to follow my instinct. I was glad to be able to help someone heal so that he could move forward, even if it meant raising a few eyebrows along the way.

On another occasion, one of my friends, Pat, was chairing a big event. She woke up the morning of the event feeling sick. She called me.

"Jane, you're going to have to do this for me," she said.

I told her about the hair conditioner and mayonnaise treatment. "A few drops of hair conditioner on your tibias and a few drops of mayonnaise mixed with a little water on your calves," I instructed her.

She had gone to Dr. Carrie before, so she immediately understood my suggestion. Meanwhile, I went to her house to pick up her script as the event chair. I began preparing to cover for her. I grew concerned, because I could hardly pronounce half of the names I was meant to read aloud. And I have never been great at speaking in front of large crowds. I was in deep trouble. And besides, this was *her* thing—she was always so wonderful at it. So, while I was reading over the script, I set the intention that she would get better (both for her sake and, selfishly, for my own). The morning of the event, a group of friends who were also close to Pat had previous plans to meet for breakfast. When we got together, I implored them to visualize Pat as being healthy, chairing the event in front of all those people. Sure enough, she got better and did a beautiful job as the event chair, as she always did.

The most important component of healing—no matter what form it takes—is to be a *part* of it, to take an active role in the process. Sometimes, it means breaking the rules to adapt the treatment or remedy to one's unique needs and philosophies. Other times, it means putting one's full faith behind the method—*knowing* that it will work versus simply *hoping* that it will. Do not lose your power to the chemo drip—own your healing, and release your fear. I try to remember that whatever is in my highest good will happen, and I acknowledge that it might not always come in the form of physical healing but possibly mental, emotional, or spiritual, too.

Both times I experienced spikes in my heart rate and blood pressure and a loss of breath, I refrained from panicking. Surely, these are scary occurrences, but somehow, I knew that panicking would only aggravate the attack. I managed to let go of fear and focused on what I had the power to do for myself, which was to focus on breathing air into my body and to set the intention to be well.

We must know that this, the ability to release fear, is possible for anyone and everyone. The right healing method is out there for each one of us, and it is important to remember that it is not always physical. When we focus on our conscious choices, it is easier to let go of fear and move forward on our chosen healing path.

It is worth noting that I never tell anyone to "do as I do." I am more aligned with the idea that "If you do as I say, you are doing it wrong," as the saying goes. It all goes back to the principle of continuously adapting advice to one's own healing path. I do what I do because of my mindset and my sensitivities, but others may find healing in conventional medicine or other forms.

I once visited a former student's mother at the cancer clinic, where she was getting her chemotherapy treatment. I walked into the room expecting to feel grim, but I was surprised to see that everyone there seemed to be filled with hope. I have heard many success stories of chemotherapy, and I do not judge anyone for pursuing whatever form of medicine he or she feels will nurture healing.

I share what works. I've developed a database of knowledge from years of reading and researching. I have been through my share of homeopathic trials and errors, but the truth is that everyone is different. Everyone has different sensitivities and reactions, and even those change over time. Today, my healing regime remains fluid based on the state of my body and mind. I borrow pages from any and all sources that align with my beliefs. There are some methods I know to be effective in other people, but not in myself, and there are some methods that have worked for me and not others. When it comes to healing, each person must follow his or her own belief system.

I know of many things I can easily teach that I don't do myself. There are many people who have healed themselves through food, for example, but in my case, there are other ways. It's about knowing one's body.

For me, ice cream would be hard to give up.

5

Mindful Medicine

We underestimate our body's ability to heal itself.
—Dr. Carrie

In a sense, I did not choose this path to healing; it chose me. In those first years of teaching, after failure upon failure in doctors' offices and hospitals, something gave way, and it turned out to be one of the most important evolutions in my wellness paradigm. I reached a point where I had nothing to lose; my body had rejected everything else. The courses of treatment prescribed by my doctors were limited at best. I felt powerless, afraid, and dependent on a system that was failing me.

I set out to break the cycle. With the help of Dr. Carrie and other practitioners, I developed a new healing philosophy rooted in alternative therapies and the power of human consciousness.

Perhaps this shift was prompted by too many experiences in a dispassionate medical environment, where a doctor saw my symptoms rather than seeing me as a whole person. I always sought a deeper connection with my physicians, and if I couldn't find one, I would look elsewhere.

So often, we find ourselves left out of the healing process. We forget that the most powerful healing source lies within ourselves. A person may sit in a doctor's office and take everything he says at face value, without questioning what makes sense for us as unique individuals. Or perhaps we place unwavering faith on the case studies that prove one thing or another, and as a result, we might neglect the truths about our wellbeing that cannot be proven but that are nonetheless critical to our healing.

I have learned over the years to approach illness as an opportunity for breakthrough. As difficult as it may be, I resist wallowing in discouragement, and I abstain from seeking out sympathy from others. When we are in a weakened state, we must be conscious of where we are sending our mental and emotional energy. When feeling sick or diagnosed with a disease, people may ask, "Why me? Why this?" To me, these reactions of self-pity, anger, and remorse only serve to reinforce the illness.

I select to dismiss many diagnoses and prognoses because I want to avoid sending my energy to the vulnerable areas. I don't even like to say the word *cancer* to describe illness because of its negative connotation. (I call it "prunie" instead, which invokes laughter instead of fear). I choose to surround myself with physicians that remain as positive and optimistic as I do. I seek out chances to introduce lightheartedness and humor into medical environments. Laughter, compassion, and child-like playfulness are often the most powerful states of consciousness to override feelings of fear and discouragement.

When I was taking Ted to FoxChase in Philadelphia for his radiation, we always made it fun. We would couple it with a show, a dinner with friends, even an overnight stay at the Hampton Inn.

Ted once said, "If I didn't know any better, I would think we were on a holiday."

Uncovering Alternatives

If the first step is to reshape how we view ourselves as patients, then the very next one is to seek empowerment through knowledge. While I continued to see my doctors and genuinely listened to their guidance, I was simultaneously educating myself on alternatives and supplements to the conventional methods. I kept an open mind. I would study the respective illness and its conventional treatment options. I read books and poured over case studies. But from there, rather than reeling in one of the options, I cast the net wider. In the words of my friend Pat, my "antenna is always up for new ideas."

I studied traditional Eastern healing techniques; I explored philosophies in anthroposophy and vibrational medicine; I discovered the practices of craniosacral, Reiki, and homeopathy. When I read something that spoke to me, I called the author. I wanted to feel the connection with the work.

And then, with an open mind and a will toward healing, I experimented. Not everything worked. Not everything failed. Over the years, gradually and with the help of a growing network of practitioners and healers whom I trusted, I developed healing methods based on the successes and failures. Perhaps my timeframe was faster than others because of my many "opportunities" to test the theories. I tried my best to keep my chin up and appreciate the process of discovery.

When I settled on a course of action that I felt aligned with my body and my healing paradigm, I put my full faith behind it. I gently released any doubts from my mind. It is so important to position ourselves in the right spiritual state of mind. The body must be at peace in order to *accept* healing.

To this day, with any form of healing that I choose, I do not *hope* that it will work - I *know* it will. It will work as long as I am to be here. I remind myself of the fact that, by default, the human body wants to repel illness. As in all organisms, evolution has equipped us with natural lines of defense. Homeopathy and many forms of alternative medicine are focused on triggering these innate defenses, whether by physiological means or—most critically—by conscious effort. I do not always have the answer, and there are times when I need to learn more about a trouble I am facing, or dig deeper to find the root cause of it. I always ask "Why?" because if something is not healing, I know there is a higher reason for it. It may serve to teach me an important lesson. Our role is merely to supply our bodies with the resources they need to thrive. That means approaching healing in a mindful way. In designing our own path, not only do we have the advantage of tailoring the regimen to our unique needs and preferences, but we also benefit emotionally and mentally by lessening fear of the unknown. Taking greater ownership of our healing methods promotes empowerment over fear and enables our conscious minds to work for us rather than against us.

Anthroposophy

Early in our relationship, I asked Dr. Carrie to define what she does. Her answer was *anthroposophical medicine.*

That was a big word, so I researched it. Anthroposophy is the study of the innate wisdom of humanity. It is the quest to methodically understand and explain human consciousness, intuition, and imagination with the rigorousness of the natural sciences. It is the scientific exploration of our inner world.

Early in my research, I found an article by Richard Leviton titled "The Promise of Anthroposophical Medicine." In the article, there were several passages that enlightened my quest. It was here that I learned more about Rudolf Steiner, the pioneer in the research and application of anthroposophy in medicine.

Steiner was an Austrian philosopher who was most known for his "Philosophy of Freedom," which presented a theory on the concept of free will and independent thinking. He became interested in exploring spirituality, and he ultimately split from the Eastern-oriented schools of thought to embrace spirituality within Christianity and the natural sciences.

In one of his dissertations entitled "Truth and Knowledge," he wrote: "The most important problem of all human thinking is this: to comprehend the human being as a personality grounded in him or herself." (Peter Schneider, *Einführung in die Waldorfpädogogik.* Schneider quotes here from Steiner's dissertation, *Truth and Knowledge).*

To Steiner, the quest to understand human nature was tied to introspection—it could be achieved individually through meditation, perception, imagination, and intuition. It was a journey into one's own mind, strictly uninhibited by outside rules, impressions, and authorities.

He believed that the inquiry into human nature was sadly abandoned with the discovery of the scientific method and our overriding interest in explaining our material world. But what of our nonmaterial world? What of our evolution in consciousness? Anthroposophy was Steiner's exploration of the answers to these questions.

Anthroposophical medicine, then, applies our knowledge of human nature to our medical practices. It seeks to marry the intricacies of human consciousness with the individual quest for healing. It is an integrative, holistic view of health and well-being.

Dr. Otto Wolff was one of the researchers who picked up where Steiner had left off in exploring the application of anthroposophy in medicine. In 1982, Dr. Wolff wrote, "Medicine will be broadened by a spiritual conception of man to an art of healing, or else it will remain a soulless technology that removes only symptoms. Through the concrete inclusion of the spirit and soul of man, a humanization of medicine, as it was inaugurated by Rudolf Steiner, is possible." (Richard Leviton, "The Promise of Anthroposophical Medicine").

To me, anthroposophical medicine points to an inner knowing. It is a way for each person to engage in his or her own healing. Each one of us is capable of being well, whole, and perfect in mind, body, and spirit. It remains up to us to find the best answers for our being. Sometimes, an illness is meant to propel us further on our chosen path. Illness can be there to teach us which aspects of our consciousness need attention. It is a gift—an opportunity for transformation—if we choose to see it in this light.

The question of healing has to do with a patient's affinity for introspection. The patient's willingness to enter a realm of self-exploration often serves as a precursor to his or her success in the medical environment.

Perhaps the physician Dr. Philip Incao said it best when he wrote: "Anthroposophical medicine is not trying to revert to ancient traditions or herbalism or faith healing, but to leaven medicine's deductive/scientific method with spiritual insight."[1]

Vibrational Healing and Homeopathy

Vibrational medicine is a concept that encompasses a large part of my healing. Two of my trusted healers, Dr. Carrie and Terry Ross, always believed that physics had more to do with healing than biology did, and I would assume that most of my healing mentors, including Rich Work, would agree with that philosophy. We all have immeasurable energies that have a large role in our health and well-being, whether physical, mental, or spiritual. Vibrational medicine is a form of healing that works on the nonphysical forces; that is, it is centered on the metaphysical. Metaphysical energy comes with many names; *chi* might be the most common one, which means "life force" in traditional Chinese medicine. Many alternative medicines, including Ayurveda, acupuncture, and Reiki, are based on the theory that health depends on these energy fields.

One aspect of vibrational medicine is the concept that "like repels like." That is, a bath or topical remedy of a substance you are trying to withdraw from your body could help remove it from your system. For example, to help deter mosquitos, one may take a bath in five pounds of sugar in order to help draw sweetness out of the body. In general, baths should last thirty minutes and should be used with only one substance in them at a time. If baths are not possible, foot baths work fine, too. Yogurt, which is made up of good bacteria, pulls bacteria out of the body. I have seen yogurt used topically for everything from thrush in the mouth to the healing of blemishes.

Dr. C's principles are centered on homeopathy, which is the concept that "like attracts like," and vibrational medicine, which is the idea that the vibrations of certain matter can be transferred to the human body. From reading Dr. Masaru Emoto's books and research, I learned about the connection between vibrations and the human consciousness. I do things to incorporate positive vibrations into my body and psyche; for instance, I put stickers on my water bottles that have different values on them, such as "energy," "gratitude," or "tranquility." I believe that the vibrations of the words are carried into the water that I drink.

Iodine is a recurring substance in my healing methods because of its cleansing properties. I float two unopened bottles of iodine in my baths to boost my immune system before traveling. I feel it helps prevent infections. I also use direct applications of iodine for healing scrapes and cuts. When I tripped and split my knee open while at the Green Valley pool, the advice I received from the nurse who came rushing over to help me was, "Go straight to the ER." She did not want to touch it. Ted looked at me; he knew what I was thinking, and we both left for home. At home, I continued to pour iodine on the cut several times a day until it healed. It is not to say that this course of action is best for everyone—I use it as an example of one of the many times I followed what I know to be best for my body. The most important rule is to follow your own conscious—your own inner knowing.

Baking soda and mustard are two of my "wonder drugs" that I use frequently. Baking soda is known to help pull acid out of and off the skin of the body, while mustard is known to pull out debris and reduce inflammation. I take a page from the wisdom of my parents' generation, who did things like mustard plasters, mustard on the skin to help relieve chest colds and inflammation in the body. Mustard contains turmeric, a natural anti-inflammatory

Once, when Ted and I were on a bus traveling up the Canyons in Utah, a woman stepped on the bus who had tripped and hurt her rib cage badly. The bus driver wanted to get her to the ER. When I heard the news, I looked at Ted. He gave me the all-knowing nod, surely aware of what I wanted to do to help the woman. I walked back to her seat and kneeled beside her. I asked her, "Do you remember our parents' mustard plasters?"

When she responded that she was familiar with them, I asked her, "Okay, then, could I smear mustard on your side to help with the swelling?" I had kept my mustard packet from the lunch box we had been given, never knowing when it might come in handy. This was generally my protocol.

She gave me the green light.

I remember a doctor and his wife sitting across from us on the bus. The doctor asked Ted what I was doing, and when Ted explained, the doctor seemed to understand immediately. "Oh, okay," he responded in agreement. That night, the woman came to dinner and proudly showed how well her side had been healing.

Olive oil is a natural healing agent with its vitamin B6 component and I use it regularly by rubbing it on troubled areas of my body. Spreading Vitamin E skin oil (the skin oil is thinner and more spreadable than the straight oil) on the body helps prevent radiation during X-rays. I have turned to these remedies time and time again to heal various health problems, injuries, and ailments, and they have worked for me, as I *know* they will.

When digestive and bowel problems occur together, Dr. Carrie instructed me to put a couple of drops of hair conditioner on my tibias, or shin bones, in addition to a couple of drops of mayonnaise and water on my calves. She told me to repeat this process ten times, one hour apart each. But, there were times, when I had to adjust the timing. At that time, I made sure to set the intent that it will work. This is the key component of all of my healing—whether I am adapting a remedy or not—the most important aspect is to not just believe, but to *know* that it will heal.

I set the intention that the healing will be done in divine perfection, even when I know I cannot do it perfectly myself. If it is to heal, it will, unless there is something else I am to learn.

Therapies that work on the metaphysical realm—that is, beyond the physical level of the body—are alternative for the very reason that they focus on aspects of wellness and healing that conventional medicine does not or cannot reach. They can work as a compliment to conventional medicine, as a supplement, or as an alternative based on the individual's health status, preferences, and philosophies.

Color Therapy

When I was asked to give my friend's eulogy, I summoned the congregation to breathe deep, steady breaths and visualize the color blue for peace and white for unconditional love. They closed their eyes and slowly took deep, even breaths as they concentrated on visualizing these colors and their meanings. After a few moments, I asked everyone to open their eyes. Some of the reactions and facial expressions were interesting, to say the least. I was not the only one to notice the overwhelming vibration of these energies in the room. A similar experience occurred at a different occasion when I asked people to visualize yellow for joy.

Color visualization has been a powerful healing tool in my life. I am thankful to Ann Marie for teaching me the philosophy of Symmetry, which is my guiding source for color therapy. Color is simply a form of visible light, of electromagnetic energy. In nature, birds and insects are drawn to certain colors, which represent for them a matter of survival. Humans are no different. We are drawn to certain colors that speak to our energies and represent the many facets of our life's journey.

Color therapy is a way to restore balance in our auras and achieve what is known as *Symmetry*. Auras are the energy fields surrounding us. There are layers of color within our auras that represent our spiritual, mental, and physical nuances. The colors that are lacking represent a void within our energy that may need more focus. By visualizing the colors we need to strengthen, our energy fields can achieve symmetry.

For instance, when I wish to strengthen my immune system, I use the color violet, which represents strength. I visualize the color blue, which stands for peace, at the back of my neck, the atlas, and I visualize red, for harmony, at the base of my spine. Then, I visualize the colors blending together throughout my spine to create violet. According to Symmetry, violet is the color that supports the immune system.

In the practice of Symmetry, all of the colors in the spectrum carry unique healing properties and are associated with a unique part of the body. The color for peace is blue, love is white, and red is harmony. Some people also consider red to represent empowerment. Yellow represents joy. Green is for balance. Orange is for creativity, and so on. The set of healing colors can be explored through the teachings, books, and Harmonics website (www.harmonicsinternational.com). I was taught the colors through their classes and became an instructor in 2002.

There are many ways for color to enrich our lives. When I go out with my two close friends, Ellen and Mary, we always wear wild colors. We laugh, we cry, we share everything. For us, the colors represent openness, eccentricity, our free spirits. It is so important for us to incorporate color into our lives.

If each one of us were to go through color visualizations and radiate our love and peace outward using the colors white and blue, the world would be a better place. Symmetry, to me, is about all things coming together to work as one, connecting and balancing mind, body, and spirit in perfect, unconditional love—what I call *divine love.*

When I was diagnosed with "prunie," Dr. Carrie fortunately connected me with the work of Ann Marie and Rich Work, starting with Rich's book, *Awaken to the Healer Within.* The proclamations in Rich Work's books have been powerful in my healing journey, and I continue to use them to this day. Their website features books, color therapy resources, audios, and essences for all interested in exploring their work further. Their definition of Symmetry is an empowerment of self-healing and transformation using the power of divine love.

Reiki Healing

Reiki is a Japanese word deriving from two concepts: *Rei*, meaning universal, and *ki*, meaning life-force energy. It was a practice developed by Mikao Usui in Japan nearly a century ago. It is a series of exercises that leverage the body's life-force energies to heal, balance, relax, and restore the body.

Reiki is a concept of working peace and harmony into each of the body's cells to allow for the healing process to begin. Practitioners view the body as a whole rather than as separate parts. Reiki healing seeks to detect and uncover underlying causes for ailments and ultimately remove those blockages so that the body's natural healing processes can take hold. The underlying premise of Reiki is that the body has evolved to want to reject illness. When we remove blockages within our bodies, we allow for the natural healing process to take hold.

Reiki uses a technique called palm healing or hands-on healing. This universal healing energy flows through the Reiki healer's palms to the patient's body. The practice aligns with the seven major chakras of the human body. Through intuition, the practitioner can sense where blockages are and focus more specifically on the areas in need of energy. The hand positions bring about various energizing effects on the physical, mental, emotional, and energetic level.

The major difference between Westernized and traditional versions of Reiki is that the former focuses on the body as a whole, whereas the latter concentrates on specific areas in need of healing. Breathing exercises are a large part of traditional Reiki as well, as the breath is thought to be a cleansing mechanism for our body and spirit.

Traditional Reiki practitioners, whose methods are rooted in Mikao Usui's direct teachings, have an intuitive sense of where to place their hands on the body for healing. When Reiki was translated for Western use, the idea of preset hand placements was welcomed so that people could learn and practice Reiki themselves.

For me, Reiki is a way to clear the energy in my body and enable the healing process to begin. I use it to clear the energy field that surrounds me. I have completed two levels of Reiki training, and it has served me well. For example, if I have knee pain, I will cup my knee and bring energy to it for healing. I have always insisted on having a Reiki master with me in the room during any significant surgeries or procedures, and I ask that the Reiki master focus his or her energy on the doctors in the room rather than on me.

Kinesiology and Pendulums

I have learned to use my body as a guide for questions on what would be best for it. A foundation for this practice is kinesiology. Kinesiology therapy is grounded on the principle that we can use muscle movement as a way to understand larger stress points in one's body. Kinesiology therapy uses muscle testing to detect blockages related to overall health and helps remove those blockages through muscle reflexes as well as other courses of therapy.

We can leverage kinesiology as a guide to helping us understand what our body wants or needs. This way of using my body came years after Dr. Carrie taught me how to use a physical pendulum. I refer to this practice as my internal pendulum. To tap into it, I stand with my feet shoulder-width apart. I quiet my mind and body for a few minutes. I ask the three questions that I learned from a healer friend of mine, Terry Ross: "May I?" (Is it okay with the powers at be?); "Should I?" (Is this the right time?); and "Can I?" (Am I up to it?). I also ask these same three questions when using an external pendulum. Three yes's means proceed—I may use my body in search of my answer. Then, I try to feel where my body gravitates. My muscles will propel me in a certain direction so long as I am in tune with my body.

Tapping Therapy

I connected with Tapping Therapy when I lost a dear friend. Our STARS group chipped in and bought a set of DVDs, which we were able to share with others thanks to the permission we received from Gary Craig, the founder of the original program. I was looking for something that others could learn easily while dealing with stress, depression and doubt. This is a combination of alternative medicine including acupuncture, neuron-linguistic programming, energy and thought field therapy. I have used this wonderful program and found it helpful for many people of all ages. The websites are included in the Additional Resources of this book. Another great resource for tapping therapy is Nick Ortner's book, The Tapping Solution, and his website, which is also listed at the end of this book.

***

While I have found success in many ways, perhaps the most critical point in my life's story is that I am not unique in my capacity for self-healing. I was not endowed with a special gift other than my curiosity for learning about my mind and body. Each one of us has the potential to start an adventure in self-awareness. It often turns into a self-fulfilling prophecy: as we make small discoveries about ourselves, we begin to yearn for the answers to bigger questions.

I could fill this book with stories of people who have met illness with a determination to understand why it was brought into their lives and a vision to overcome it. These are the same people who go off to publish books, compose symphonies, and discover the next medical breakthroughs. So often, they champion their illness or trauma for furnishing them with a new worldview, an invigorated sense of self, an appreciation for all that life has to offer.

My sensitivities prompted me to find answers outside of the treatments conventional doctors had always prescribed, and so I turned to alternative methods. I put on my "student" hat and found consolation in the lessons that each hardship brought. I accepted each illness as an opportunity to learn.

And thank goodness I did. As I started going down the path of alternative medicine, I realized that I was meant to discover this form of healing. The knowledge I had gained from previous trials would serve as the primary resource as I navigated my life's next chapter—and the biggest challenge I had yet to face.

6

Dissolving Fear

Whatever is for our highest good will happen.

The breast lump had come out of nowhere. It hadn't been there the day before. So when Ted and I woke up one morning to find the egg-sized form on the left side of my left breast, I knew that it wasn't *mine*. In fact, when I discovered the lump, my first thought was, *No problem, I'll just get rid of it.*

The night before, I had taken on the anguish of a friend. She had sought my guidance for some time since the death of her daughter. She was seeking answers to questions yet unresolved. I spent hours on the phone with her that night. The conversation ran late, and eventually, we had to end it. I fell asleep.

The very next morning, I woke up to discover the lump in my breast, the mysterious mass that hadn't been there before. I knew immediately what it was. My friend's sorrow had manifested itself in me. I thought, *I've taken this on for her. She won't have to deal with her pain anymore.*

No problem. It's not mine. I'll just get rid of it.

Because I had spent time researching homeopathy, vibrational medicine, and anthroposophy, and then testing those theories on my own body, I was feeling secure in my ability to heal through alternative methods. I had a deep relationship with my inner self. I believed I was at the point in my life where I could confidently enter any health problem without fear. Whatever would be, would be.

For the first several months after my discovery of the breast lump, I pursued my own path to healing. I was receiving positive signs and affirmations as to my progress. But a friend had been begging me to get a professional opinion. After several months of hesitation, I did.

And then, as if in a whirlwind, I found myself seated in a surgeon's office, facing a chart with stages on it.

His hands moved from the beginning stage to the next one, the next one, and the last one, where he stopped with a grim expression. He would then inform me that the operation indicated infiltrating lobular carcinoma, and that the cancer was much more aggressive than he had initially thought.

"You will need to undergo intensive radiation, chemotherapy, and tamoxifen if you're to have any chance of surviving," he said. "Following this prescription will give you a few more months. You will need to act fast."

I will never forget that moment, sitting in that chair, staring at that chart, entering a state of profound fear for the first time since my twenties. It felt as though something inside of me was freezing up—something beyond my control was challenging everything I thought I knew. What my spiritual world had been indicating to me over the past several months was being threatened. The prognosis hit me hard as stone.

"If there's anybody out there who's telling you they can heal you, they are lying to you," my surgeon cautioned. He knew that I was embedded in the world of alternative healing. He handed me a book on breast cancer with a scowl on his face.

In this paralyzing fear, all I wanted to do was get out the door. I stood up from my chair and left the office.

When I made it home, the cancer book promptly found its way to the trash bin. I reached for an indication that would quiet my fears and reassure my initial conviction that my body would be able to heal itself. I cleared my mind, and then I asked for a sign.

When I received it (in fact, I received two), I gently released that fear and chose to deny its surfacing into my psyche again.

***

When we discovered the lump, my first reaction was that it couldn't be anything but a fibroid tumor or something that I was going to be able to get rid of easily.

The Sunday after we found it, Ted and I were at Unity Church. We always formed around a circle and sang a peace song, "Let There Be Peace on Earth." In that moment while we were singing, I started feeling a unique sensation. I felt something strange come over my body. I knew I had to leave.

I signaled to Ted, and we left together. We didn't go straight home, because we needed to stop and pick up some last-minute things for our trip to Las Vegas to visit our son and daughter-in-law the following week. We stopped at Sam's Club. We were walking around getting our groceries, and as we were standing in line for the register, everything in front of me started getting hazy and shaky. My sight filled with brilliant colors: yellow, purple, red, green, and blue. The haze grew thicker, and suddenly, I couldn't see Ted. I looked around and realized I couldn't see anyone or anything in the store. I reached out for Ted's hand and, ever so calmly, clued him in.

"Ted, I can't see you, and I can't stand up," I said under my breath. "I don't know what's wrong."

He led me over to a chair, where I sat down to rest.

The cashier had overheard our conversation and called her manager over to us. They asked if they should call an ambulance to get me to the hospital. I politely declined. Whatever it was, I had a sense it would clear from my system.

Ted helped me into the car and drove us home. By the time we arrived, my vision was starting to return, but I was still feeling weak and shaky.

I wanted to understand what was happening to me. I reached for the phone and dialed my friend Terry Ross. Terry was a profoundly spiritual person. I trusted him for advice because I had always felt a deep connection with him.

I felt I might be able to find an answer from Terry, so I called him for guidance. When he picked up, I asked him if he could see anything related to the lump I had discovered in my breast.

His answer was immediate and decisive. "I can't find any cancer in your body, Jane. I just don't see it there at all."

I felt moved by his response. Terry was a dowser: he helped people find water and oil based on a sense he had. He was so strongly connected with the earth that he could identify areas of pollution and places that had histories of conflict, just by spiritually connecting to those spaces. He felt the imprint of those conflicts were still there physically. He helped villages in developing countries find water, never asking for anything in return. Often, he would do this spiritually without even being there in person. He felt he was meant to use his sense and his connection to the earth to help those in need. At his invitation-only memorial service, there were doctors from prestigious hospitals sharing stories about Terry and how he had helped several of their patients through health issues, even when the doctors themselves did not understand an illness. People read letters sent from villages all over the world thanking him for sharing his gifts.

Considering how deeply connected Terry was with the natural world, I felt that his answer about my diagnosis was true. I contemplated his words: *I can't find cancer in your body, Jane. I just don't see it there at all.*

When I called my healer, Dr. Carrie, her answer was the same. "I don't see anything like cancer in your body," she affirmed.

Her interpretation of the lump went a step further.

"What happens," she explained, "is that, after years of having pneumonia at least twice a year for as many as ten years like you have, the debris from the illness collects in our bodies in different places."

She went on to explain that, in my case, my body was strong enough to have cleansed the debris from my lungs, which were essential, but it needed somewhere to go, and so it collected in a nonessential place, my breast.

"My apologies to Ted," said Dr. Carrie, "but you do not need your breasts as much as you need your lungs."

The affirmations from my spiritual friends validated what I was already feeling—that the lump was nothing to worry about. I had faith that I could heal it on my own. Then I received a powerful message from a friend of mine, Michael Schuster, who was an intuitive. Michael said to me, "Jane, you will know by the end of March whether you are to live or die from this."

On the very last day of March, I came home to a voicemail message on my machine from Rich Work, who did not know Michael Schuster or what Michael had said to me. The message from Rich said, "Jane, I just want you to know that you are not going to die now." It represented yet another form of verification for me that it was not my time to leave. I was fortunate to discover the book *Awaken to the Healer Within*, which essentially opened my world further to self-healing.

Per my usual course of action, I originally worked with Dr. Carrie to develop natural treatments. But a few weeks of treatments would come and go without a change in the size or shape of the lump. I took a moment to resolve to myself: *If nothing changes by September, then I will see a conventional doctor.*

It was April. Over the course of the next five months, life would begin to challenge my confidence, slowly and subtly at first, and then gradually more intensely, until it culminated with the cancer chart and the deepest place of fear.

The first alarm came when I left with Ted and his brother and sister-in-law, Bruce and Betty, to visit with our son Robb in Las Vegas. I was startled when Robb told me he had the strange feeling he was not going to see someone again. Knowing what I was facing, I thought he was tapping into my problem. As it turns out, he was channeling another omen, as Betty died unexpectedly a month after our trip.

Then there was the trip to Ireland. I was always scanning airfare deals, and when I found an unbelievable first-class price to fly to Ireland, I booked the trip. Considering my uncertainty around my health, I felt compelled to visit my father's homeland.

A few days before we left for the trip, I had another conversation with Terry Ross. He told me that there were two specific places in Ireland I should avoid. One area was around Castle Leslie in the north, and the other around Limerick in the south, including the small town of Adare. He told me that these were places with ancient, complicated, and chaotic energies for me. He saw sensitivity in me, and considering the lump, he cautioned that it would not be wise of me to go near them unprotected.

We took off for the trip with two other couples that were close to us, and we were having a wonderful time. We had plans to visit Castle Leslie. Even though I had been cautioned against it, I felt safe traveling to the site as long as I was conscious of it. I protected myself with positive energy, which I felt acted as a shield against any negative energy in the area. We visited the castle, and I was feeling good.

As the trip went on, I was so enthralled by the country and its beautiful landscapes and warm and friendly people that the warning of Limerick slipped to the back of my mind. Incidentally, Limerick is where we had planned to finish the trip.

We visited an old, stone church in Adare, which was in the Limerick area. Adare is a replica of an ancient village similar to the style of Williamsburg, Virginia. In the church, there was a copy of the Pieta. As I walked toward it, I looked around at the old, stone walls of the church. It was as if these stones were talking to me. I asked Ted if he would take a photo of the Pieta. He stepped toward it. As he took the photo, I felt a rush come over me. Suddenly, it was as if all of my life-force energy was leaving my body. I collapsed.

Many times in my life, stones, especially in churches, have triggered a reaction in me. I feel that they carry certain vibrations, certain emotions that they have been exposed to in the past. Years later, I went into a meditation seeking the reason behind my strong reaction to church stones. I learned that I had, in a past life, died in a church. I was killed because I witnessed something that I was not meant to see. This is the reason why old, stone churches have always instilled strong emotional and physical reactions in me, and I believe it is the reason why I experienced what I did that day in Adare.

When I awoke, Ted was helping me out of the church. He led me across the dirt path to a small linen shop across the way. In the shop, I clung to a table. I concentrated on breathing into my body. I tried to regain my consciousness and my physical strength.

The very next day, I woke up and checked the lump. It had grown to nearly twice its original size. Once again, my faith in my self-healing process was splintered.

***

September came, and I knew what I had to do. I had tried other ways of removing the lump on my own, but now the signs were pointing me in the direction of seeking conventional medical advice. A friend of mine convinced me to call a doctor.

"Please," she begged, "just get an opinion."

I decided to reach out to a doctor that I had seen sixteen years before at the Reading Hospital, whom I had been pleased with at the time. He wasn't available, so he sent me to his associate.

When I met with the doctor, he was alarmed at the size of the tumor. He examined me and then said, "This is not the typical breast cancer."

Beyond that, I hardly remember the conversation. I stopped listening from the moment he told me, quite irritated, that he only had twelve minutes to spend with me. What he was telling me was not important. At this point, I was in a state of denial.

The doctor prescribed a mammogram.

Promptly and politely, I declined.

"I don't do them," I simply said.

"Elderly lady who does not listen." I could see this was the note he wrote in his records. (Later, I received my records with this note, and I taped it to my refrigerator.) He grew frustrated with me. Seeing that I wouldn't budge on my conviction, he offered an alternative.

"Fine," he conceded, "we can do an ultrasound."

"Okay," I responded, "I will do that."

The week before the ultrasound appointment, I happened to develop a rash on the inside of my arm. To me, its shape resembled that of a flying whale. When I went in for the ultrasound and the doctor projected my lump on the screen, it looked to be the same shape—that of a flying whale. It looked as if the shape of my rash had literally imprinted itself on my breast.

"Oh, look!" I exclaimed, startling the doctor. "I have a flying whale on my arm!"

He was not amused by my revelation.

Based on the ultrasound results, the doctor recommended I undergo surgery to remove the breast lump. He referred me to a surgeon.

I decided to see a surgeon I was familiar with who was open to alternative techniques, Dr. Frangipane. When I met with him, he was already suggesting what I had been thinking: I wanted to have a Reiki master in the operating room with me. By this time, I had completed two levels of Reiki, and I felt that a particular attention to my energy fields would be important if I would be subjecting myself to surgery. When I engaged in this conversation with Dr. Frangipane, his openness validated that he would be the right doctor for me.

Dr. Frangipane expressed his concern about the tumor. He wanted to operate as soon as possible. He also told me that I absolutely needed to get the mammogram, EKG, and blood tests—there was no way he could operate without them. He scheduled me for the blood work and the EKG first and the mammogram a few days after that. I felt good enough in my connection with Dr. Frangipane to follow his instruction. I allowed him to schedule me for the tests.

On the day of my EKG, I was in the testing room when I noticed that Dr. Frangipane's office was right down the hall. When I finished the test, I decided to walk down to visit with him. I am usually anxious to leave hospital settings, so I don't know why I felt the urge to see him. But I did, and when I got there, I was alarmed to find that his name was no longer on the door.

I went into his office. His receptionist informed me that he had quit the practice on Monday—the first workday immediately following my visit with him. (I would never come to learn why he left the practice so suddenly.)

I took this as a sign. I left the office and opted to celebrate the natural canceling of my surgery with a strawberry-and-banana smoothie.

Ted and I had made plans to fly to Florida for a short getaway, a little escape from the stresses of my ordeal. We left for the trip as planned, and when we returned, I had a dozen messages on my machine and a letter from my surgeon's partner. Everybody was wondering where I was. They were alarmed that I would leave without notice. They insisted that I come in for my biopsy and mammogram.

At this point, I felt it was best to continue on the path I had started with Dr. Frangipane, even if it meant finding a new surgeon who I could trust. I chose not to go to his associate, and rather, I pursued the prescribed course of action with a new surgeon that a friend had recommended, Dr. G. When I met with Dr. G., I was pleased with his pleasant demeanor and openness to having a Reiki master in the operating room, even though he did not know what it was. He also agreed to do the operation as an outpatient surgery, per my request. I knew not to settle for just any doctor—I had to feel good about my choice; I had to feel a connection.

When I went in for the remaining tests, the mammogram showed that the tumor was quite large. Then, the biopsy showed carcinoma. My surgeon's direction for me was to have a lumpectomy to remove the breast tumor as well as to remove my lymph nodes.

I wanted affirmation that this was the right course of action for me. I went into meditation, seeking clarity. The message that came through to me was straightforward: I decided to have the lumpectomy, but my lymph nodes would stay.

***

In the months leading up to the operation, I wanted to continue my efforts to remove the lump in my own way, through homeopathy. The process of finding my own answers and taking action was itself intrinsically empowering. I reached out to a homeopathic doctor in Las Vegas named Dr. Royal, to whom Terry Ross had connected me.

When I went to see Dr. Royal, the first thing he asked me was, "Why are you here?" He wanted to know my reasons for seeking alternative therapy. I responded that Terry Ross had recommended him to me in light of my cancerous tumor.

"Do you believe it?" he asked me.

"No," I responded.

He repeated his original question: "So why, then, are you here?"

He explained that his work revolved around building up the immune system—he worked with patients to *prevent* illness, not treat it. His practice was grounded in chelation, a therapy that pushes fluid through the body to help pull out metals and toxins. Nonetheless, he agreed to work with me. He conducted a test that showed high levels of heavy metals, including arsenic, in my body (a recurring theme in my life), and he prescribed a series of chelation therapies to extract the metals. Then, he sent me home with seven bottles of homeopathic liquids. Each bottle was one ounce in size, and he instructed me to take specific—and differing—amounts of each one per day. He anticipated that I would need to call to order more of the liquids at some point.

I went home and pursued the course of treatment. My body had typically easily accepted homeopathics, where it usually had rejected most other medicine. Energy work, lymphatic massage, meditations, visualizations, positive intentions, and natural remedies were my main line of defense through this period. I was scheduled to undergo surgery to remove the tumor, but I also felt that I needed to take matters into my own hands to prepare myself—physically, spiritually, and mentally—as best as I could for what was to come.

As late March rolled around, I noticed something peculiar about my homeopathic bottles. I picked up one of the bottles and noticed it was half-full. I took out all of the bottles and put them on the windowsill, one by one, so I could see them better. The fluids in the bottles were all at exactly the same level—halfway full. I was shocked. I showed them to Ted.

He asked, "Jane, are you sure you've been taking all of them?"

65

"Yes, every day for months now," I explained. It seemed as though I had hardly made a dent in the supply.

Not knowing how to read this phenomenon, I called the homeopathic clinic to find out more about the liquids. When I reached Dr. Royal's assistant, I asked that she pass on the message. Then, without realizing what I was saying, I told her that it was a matter regarding loaves of bread and fish. It was the only way I found to explain it.

Shortly thereafter, Dr. Royal called me back. He asked, "Jane, what is this matter regarding loaves of bread and fish?" I told him about the unusually high levels of liquid remaining in the bottles.

He paused and then said, "I don't know why I am saying this to you, but I want you to get your Bible out. I want you to read the first eight or so verses of Isaiah 38. I don't know why I am telling you this—all I know is that you are to read it."

I was shocked that he had a response to my peculiar message to him. I opened a Bible and read the passage.

In the passage, Hezekiah, the King of Judah, is sick and nearing death. The Lord sends Isaiah to tell Hezekiah that the Lord is ready to take him, and that he should accordingly get his house in order. Hezekiah becomes upset. He prays to the Lord, explaining that his country needs him and that this is a bad time for him to leave. He prays for more time.

When the Lord hears this message, he replies, "I have heard your prayers; I have seen your tears; behold, I will add fifteen years to your life." Then the Lord indicates to Hezekiah that he will know this to be true when he sees that his sundial is turned back in time.

I was stunned, not only by the connection that Dr. Royal made with my message, but by the fact that this particular passage was analogous to a message I received a week earlier from Rich Work. Rich told me to see my life as an odometer in a car and to set it back.

"Jane, set it back to zero," he said, "and restart it."

Then he shared a passage with me entitled "Reset Your Odometer" and included a proclamation with it. "See if this makes sense to you," he said.

When I read it, it all made sense to me. The passage is paraphrased here:

> *Everyone comes into a life experience with an agenda. We come, we experience, we grow, we complete our contract, and we leave. Some call it your soul-contract. When the soul-contract is complete, we go home.*
>
> *However, we have the option to rewrite our contract and write a new script as we move forward in consciousness.*
>
> *If it is your desire to rewrite your contract to be well, whole and perfect in mind, body and soul; transmute your world into one which brings you joy and experience the celebration of life; it is time to reset your odometer. Put it in motion. Now sit down, and rewrite your contract (Rich Work, Veils of Illusion, 2002).*

I realize this message may not make sense to all. I think if I had not been on the path I had been on, I would have doubted this message. However, because of the deep regard I learned for spiritual things as well as my personal connection to Dr. Carrie and especially Rich, I had no doubt that this message was true for me.

***

On the day of the surgery, I was presented with the consent papers to sign. I saw that the lymph nodes were on it. I crossed them off and signed my name on the *X* at the bottom of the page.

At the same time, I told the Reiki master not to worry about me, but to channel her energy to the anesthesiologist and the surgeon. The operation went smoothly, and I was fortunate to be back at home in a few hours, as I had insisted on outpatient surgery. The incision was healing nicely. There wasn't even any bruising around it, which was so unusual for me, as I bruise quite easily. In fact, I was feeling so good that I started doing some things around the house. While reaching for something in the living room, I ripped open my stitches. It meant a trip back to the emergency room to get the incision butterflied.

Two days later, I went for my follow-up visit with the surgeon. He had turned out to be an excellent surgeon, and I was glad that I had trusted my intuition to choose the right person for the job. The incision had healed almost completely. The results were yet to come.

Meanwhile, I sought answers as to my fate. I had gone into meditations earlier, whose indications were promising. Whatever discussions I had with the surgeon, earlier I didn't remember. They didn't seem important. I was confident in the messages that had come through in my meditations, as well as the verifications from my healers.

But then, a week later, I went in for the big meeting. I sat down in my surgeon's office, and he pulled out a chart—*the* chart. And as I sat there and listened to the prognosis, fear overcame me. The chart had several stages on it, and according to him, I was in the last.

Knowing what would be my denial of the prognosis, the surgeon contended to the contrary.

"If you think someone else is going to heal you, you're wrong," he said to me.

***

I felt afraid, powerless, confused. I didn't understand why I was getting mixed messages—the one from my surgeon and the one in my meditations. My internal wisdom had never failed me before like this. I was so sure that the lump was benign that I had not been open to any other possibility. Suddenly, I was faced to question my entire belief system.

My surgeon's prognoses had brought me to rock bottom. But the good thing about the bottom is that there is nowhere to go but up. I pooled all of the strength I could, and I summoned my spirit. Although I could not completely remove the fear from my psyche, I was able to quiet it in order to sink more deeply into myself. I reestablished the connection between my body and my mind and my spirit.

When I regained control of my consciousness, I decided to ask the universe for help in restoring my faith. I was not seeking answers; I had already found them in my meditations. I wanted an indication that these answers were true over the ones that my surgeon had provided. As I always have done in times of fear or uncertainty, I asked for a sign.

Solace came when I received two in the twenty-four hours after receiving my prognosis.

The evening of the prognosis, we went home and turned on the television. Ted was going around the dials. He passed the PBS station, where Dr. Wayne Dyer appeared. I told him to stop; I wanted to hear what he was saying.

Dr. Dyer was talking about his daughter, who had marks on her face that made her feel embarrassed. Everywhere her parents took her for medical guidance, the answer was the same: "You'll grow out of them," they all said. She was very unhappy—she wanted them off of her face immediately. Her parents finally took her to a doctor who gave her a powerful suggestion.

The doctor saw how upset the girl was over her facial marks. So he said to her, "I want to tell you something. You must not just *believe*; you must *know* that they will be gone from your face." That night, her parents couldn't find her anywhere in the house. They finally found her upstairs under a blanket, shining a flashlight on her face.

She was saying aloud to herself, "I believe and I *know* that they will be gone."

Dr. Dyer concluded the program with the outcome that, within a few days, the marks on her face had disappeared.

This was my first sign. It was a clear message to me that I should have faith in my own answers. I must not only believe—I must *know* that they are true, as they have always been.

When I woke up the next morning, my spirits had already been lifted. I was looking around the house for a box that could fit a few things I was planning on shipping to my cousins in Ireland. I couldn't find one of the right size.

Ted came in the door. He had gone out to get the morning paper and asked if I had seen the box that was on the front step. I had not. He grabbed it and brought it in. It was an empty cardboard box, and it happened to be the exact size box I needed. Where had it come from? This was a question without an answer. In that very moment, with this humble sign, my inner knowing resurfaced. It was my second confirmation. It was the answer I needed to evolve from *believing* that I would be well to truly *knowing* it. The difference between them is critical. I knew I was meant to continue on my own path to healing, and I felt empowered in this truth from that day forward.

It was with these signs that my fear dissolved. Had I not found a place of peace and openly asked for the answers, I would not have been perceptive enough to detect the subtle signs that eliminated my fear.

With this information, it was easy to let the doctor know where I stood during our third and final meeting. I would find my own natural treatments, I told him.

His reaction was interesting. I sensed he was in denial of my response. He asked Ted to come into the room, and he spoke to Ted as if I was not even there. He went on to explain what needed to be done if I was to have any more time to live: chemotherapy, radiation, and tamoxifen, he advised.

As we left the office, Ted asked me, "Jane, what do you really want to do?"

"Go to Friendly's for a hot fudge sundae," I replied.

And my husband, honoring my wishes as he always has, took me to Friendly's for a hot fudge sundae.

There are so many things to which we can gravitate for empowerment and self-healing. I believe in signs, but in truth, we can use almost anything to help us cope with hardship, simply by assigning a designation that represents something positive.

Each person must follow his or her own belief system. If someone feels chemotherapy will work, it will work for him or her as best as it can. The most important aspect of healing is to enter it without fear, whether it is a conventional, alternative, or simply a psychological treatment.

This is the most difficult barrier for someone to overcome, but it is the most important, as fear will block our body's healing abilities. Fear keeps people stuck in a place where they cannot see beyond what is feared. It is fear that keeps people from staying true to themselves. It is fear that prevents an individual from taking the course of action that is best for him or her. When people have fear, they are controlled by a force other than themselves.

Something as simple as word associations can cause real fear or stress in someone. I stopped using the *c* word to describe cancer long ago because of what the word triggers in the body—mainly, fear. My suggestion for any illness is to start by giving it a different name.

And then, quiet the mind and ask for guidance. Whatever answers we need will come to us, as long as we ask the right question and remain open to the response. The guideposts are there for us when we need to find our way.

When I asked for a sign relating to my prognosis, I resisted the urge to ask, *Will I survive?*

Instead, I reminded myself of the answers I had already discovered on my own. And then I asked, *Do my answers remain true?*

The signs I perceived did not indicate to me that I would survive— they purely reinforced my inner knowing that I had already chosen to do so.

"Transmuting Fears"

From the Divine Love that flows within my Being,
I forgive all my fears and all my reactions to those fears.
I transmute them into the divine expression of Creative Love
And integrate them into my wholeness in peace, joy and
harmony for all.
And so it is.

From *Proclamations of the Soul* by Rich Work, 1999.

7

The Power of Thought

I am: two of the most powerful words.
For what you put after them shapes your reality.
—Unknown

It was election night, November 7, 2000. The energies in the air were chaotic. I was on my way to pick up a friend and drive her to a show—a favor she had asked of me. On my way to her apartment, I hit a dirt mound that sent my car flying. In an instant, I looked out of the window and realized I was looking down onto the ground. The car was rolling out of control, until suddenly, it righted itself with a jolt.

Since my breast surgery the year before, I had not worn a seatbelt because it was not comfortable for me. When I stepped out of the car, I felt extreme pain in my right arm. I tried to lift it. It was dangling from its shoulder socket.

Ted took me to the hospital, where X-rays showed no broken bones. The doctors referred me to an orthopedic surgeon. At the surgeon's office, the MRI results were clear: I had completely torn my rotator cuff. Dr. Marchinski indicated that the only way to heal the injury was to have an operation to reattach the tendon. He set the operation date for January 15.

In the meantime, I sought healing in my own methods. I called a Reiki master and friend of mine to do energy work on me. She started on my feet to gauge where to focus her attention. As she was working, I received a message that she was meant to stop. Everything was taken care of, I felt. I could hardly finish receiving the thought in my mind when I noticed that my friend had ceased working on me. I asked her why she stopped.

"I feel I am not meant to continue," she replied assuredly.

On the day of my scheduled surgery, I was feeling calm and confident in my decision to go into the operation. The surgeon hadn't heard of Reiki, but he allowed me to have a Reiki master in the operating room, as it had brought such comfort to me before. Despite some hesitation on his part, he also permitted me to undergo the operation as an outpatient.

I laid down on the gurney and was feeling at peace when the anesthesiologist came to see me. I noticed that he had a worried look on his face. My blood pressure was registering at 220 over 110—unusual for most patients, but a perfectly standard and common bodily response for me when in the presence of doctors and hospitals.

When I learned what the anesthesiologist's concern was, I tried to explain how common it was for my blood pressure to jump to these levels—it was simply a given anytime time I was in a medical setting. As soon as I was to leave, it would drop back to normal, like clockwork. He was still worried and told his assistants to increase the anesthesia dose.

I remember pointing out the bright lights as my doctors wheeled me into the operating room.

"They're beautiful." I kept going on about the lights, as if I was high on LSD. I said, "Don't tie me down too tight. I get claustrophobic."

In my mind, I never went out, while in reality, I did. What I didn't know was that, while I was under, the doctors were able to get my blood pressure down to an appropriate level for operating, but then, as soon as they were ready to perform the surgery, it spiked again. They reached a decision point and decided the risk was too great; they would not be able to operate on me.

After some deliberation, the doctors wheeled me out of the operating room, and then something unusual happened. As soon as I was pushed beyond the threshold of the room, my blood pressure started dropping all the way back to normal. The doctor and Reiki master were stunned—they hadn't seen anything like this before. They could not continue to operate at this point because the room was taken for the next operation, and they wouldn't have time.

I was advised to begin taking blood pressure medicine so that I would be healthy for a rescheduled surgery, which was made for early March. The doctor also advised me to begin doing physical therapy exercises along with my natural routine to build up my shoulder strength.

I followed suit, attending each of my scheduled therapy sessions as advised by my doctor. The therapist gave me exercises to do at home in-between visits. When I saw him, he praised me on my progress.

"I can see you've been doing the exercises I recommended," he said to me.

Incidentally, I hadn't done as many of them as I should have, but what I *did* do faithfully was to visualize myself performing the exercises. I had firmly set my intention on healing my shoulder, and I made sure to send my energy to it with this vision in mind.

By mid-February, I was no longer in pain. I continued with visualizations, natural remedies, and the physical therapy sessions that would have been my post-operative regimen. In time, I was starting to feel so great that I decided to postpone the operation until I could consult with the surgeon. When I went in to speak with him, he was surprised by the health of my shoulder. He told me to continue with the recovery therapy and return in two months for a checkup. He said he would cancel the surgery if my shoulder continued to improve as it did.

When we met again two months later, my shoulder was nearing optimal shape. My doctor told me about a study on torn rotator cuffs that had recently been conducted. The research pointed to a subgroup of people who were able to heal a completely torn rotator cuff without surgery. He welcomed me to the group. I have a high regard for the way Dr. Marchinski recognized and honored my needs.

Mind Over Matter

My close friend Theresa was battling Guillain-Barre, a disease where the body's nervous system is attacked by antibodies. Her hands and legs were weak. She was placed in the hospital's intensive care unit and started experiencing paralysis in different parts of her body. Her outcome was cloudy.

I would visit her in the ICU, and I would take her hands in mine, stretching them out so she could see and feel them. I wanted to help her direct positive energy to her weak spots. I felt it would help her to see and feel herself healing.

"Do you see, Theresa?" I would ask her. "Do you see how you can stretch your hands like this? That is something that you can do. Focus on that." Energy work was also part of my time with her.

I knew Theresa would get better. One day, when Theresa was in rehab, I went with her granddaughters as they were leaving her room.

I said to them, "Listen, your grandmother has an incredible will to live. You know how strong she is. You must picture her in that way, okay? Not in the way the medical social worker just said."

I was certain that the combination of Theresa's strong will, her unbelievable faith, and the love and support of family and friends would propel her into recovery. I liked watching her in therapy, where she demanded as much as she could handle. There was no doubt as to her intention to be well.

The medical system was predicting that she might spend the rest of her life in a wheelchair, as some others with the disease had experienced, but she wanted to walk again, and she did. She is still very active to this day.

At the center of my philosophy on healing is mindfulness. It is a matter of recognizing the power of thought to shape our outcomes, whether in health or in any facet of our world.

I have learned to have my thoughts work in my best interest. So many of us have a deep fear of illness and death, but our energies feed it. Some people say, "I have six months to live." If they believe it, then they will.

I try to be mindful of what others are telling me is best for my body. Especially with diagnoses, it may be a doctor's perception, but it doesn't have to be mine. I can choose to own it or reject it. I usually reject it and instead form my own judgment.

In the medical world, I have always been able to find the doctors and healers I need—they have always entered my life when I seek them out. I try to find ones that are open, good listeners, and adaptive to my viewpoint. Most importantly, I ask them to think positively on my behalf. The more people with whom I can surround myself that are picturing me as well, whole, and perfect, the better.

The greatest sense of empowerment comes with knowing exactly what our body needs and opting to give it just that. There is an inner knowing within each and every one of us. I don't have anything special—everybody is in the same position. We just have to tap into the knowledge we already have. We too often negate it because we think we *should* be doing something. But our own voice is our most powerful resource. We are meant to find our own answers.

The key in my life has been learning how to bridge the connection between mind and body. It is not an easy venture. I was fortunate to begin this process at a young age. I recall asking myself at age twelve, *"What body am I in?"* I did not yet feel connected to it. Slowly, this developed with time, and like all good things, practice. Even if one's connection to his or her body has not yet been explored, it is possible.

Mindfulness begins with a recognition of the power of thought. I view my thoughts as incredibly powerful electrical currents that pulsate through my body. When I am in control of my thoughts, the potential to positively influence how the body functions and heals itself is infinite. People have been known to shrink tumors and heal wounds simply by visualizing those aims. I advise people to have their thoughts work for them, not against them. When we see ourselves as weak or ill, those energies will proliferate within us. When I pray for someone, I picture him as healthy and happy, doing what he loves to do. That is where I send my energy.

One of my fundamental mantras is "like attracts like." Positive thought will attract positive things to one's life, just as negative thought tends to turn into a self-fulfilling prophecy.

Gaining Control of Our Thoughts

When I led a stress-management workshop at the Cornwall Manor health center, I queried the group about the kinds of stress they face. Prominent answers were declining health and loss of independence. Many have a fear of death, and as we age, this becomes a source of strain and anxiety. But fear is an energy-draining emotion. And it also paralyzes us from enjoying the present. I reminded the group of the concept that we can direct our thoughts; we have the authority to fill our mind with whatever we choose. Even though declining health and death might be fearful concepts, we do not have to dwell in this emotion on a daily basis. I taught them about the power of touch and how, especially for elderly people, eyesight and hearing and taste can fade, but touch is usually the last to go. Focusing on this sensuality can help us enjoy the present and direct our thoughts toward positive things in our lives. To demonstrate the point, I handed out fuzzy teddy bears to the group, and immediately, everyone could feel the sense of joy and playfulness fill the air.

Mary Ellen, the chaplain of the retirement center, would help me push the patients' wheelchairs around as we "danced" to the music of the '30s and '40s. In their minds, the patients went to a happier time.

Rich Work taught me to simply say, "Oh, my, isn't that interesting!" when I hear or see something that I don't want to get wrapped up in. It's a simple way to avoid becoming pulled into drama or negative thought.

Our limitless energies as human beings can be directed toward negative or positive ends. Our thoughts and perceptions manifest our realities. But, often, the moments in our lives that require the most positive intention are the same ones in which we find ourselves overcome by fear or stress. How do we reconcile this predicament?

The only solution to this paradox is to practice gaining control of our thoughts. When we exercise mind control outside of those moments of fear and stress, we can tap into it when we most need to; only then will we be able to override the reckless emotions with more beneficial positive thinking.

Like all good things, it takes practice, which can take many forms, including meditation or simply focusing on breath work and the sensual experiences of touch, taste, sound, and scent. I like the sensual exercises because they are the simplest way to direct our thoughts. To purely experience the play of air on the skin or to listen for the most distant sounds is to connect the conscious mind to the physical body in a simple way, and by establishing this connection, we are learning to control the mind. The benefits are far-reaching. It is a practice in directing thought, of course, but it also helps me feel more present in my body and has the adjunct benefit of clearing my mind of other thoughts.

Meditation has also been a powerful pathway for practicing control over my thoughts. It is the most fundamental form of harnessing the mind's energy and gearing it toward a desired end. At first, the goal may simply be to quiet the mind. Learning how to gently release the "noise" is liberating in itself, and it also represents an initial capacity to control our thoughts.

It's a fancy word, and I have friends that pay all sorts of money to learn how to do it. I am sure it helps greatly, however, I feel it's so simple. All that's needed is a dedication to quieting the body and the mind. People think it has to be a long endeavor. In the beginning it may only be a matter of a couple of minutes. Then the time gets longer.. If a thought comes into my mind, I release it and push it gently away. I try not to get frustrated when my mind won't go completely blank.

It can be done in many ways: sitting, lying down, standing, and even walking. Most do it in a sitting position. When I start my meditations, I try to find a time of peace and quiet. I let go of distraction and quiet my mind. I breathe in through my nose and out through my mouth. Others do it differently, and what's important is that you set the intention before you start. For my own meditations, I set the intention to breathe in peace and breathe out anything that does not serve me. I take slow, even breaths and pay attention to the present moment without attachment to outcome or bias. It helps to be clear and release all of the tension in my body. Whenever I get distracted, I let go of it and return to the breath. Sometimes, I focus on an object or see myself on a beach watching the waves coming in and going out. Just find whatever works for you, whether that is a favorite place or simply a mantra. Perhaps there is a word that you repeat such as *love* or *peace*. I find it is important to be patient and take time in the beginning to find the best posture. You may even set a clock to keep track of your timing if you find it helpful. I often meditate in bed at night or when walking around the yard. Have faith that you can do it. In the final stage, there is the simple feeling of wakefulness, conducive to clear vision and complete awareness. It requires conscious effort to turn attention inward. With practice, the quieting of the mind becomes easier. Remember the statement: "All we seek can be found within." After meditating, I then open myself back to the world slowly.

Meditation is the active cultivation of one's mind, leading to clear awareness, tranquility, and inner wisdom. With practice, the quieting of the mind becomes easier. Then comes the opportunity to direct those thoughts not just to silence, but also to a higher end.

Visualization

The soul cannot think without a picture.
—Aristotle

The power of visualization has been shown time and again to help improve our healing on conscious and subconscious levels. When we visualize ourselves as healthy and happy, we are sending our energy toward those ends in a whole new way.

Visualization can be a powerful tool for achieving a range of goals, whether it is peace of mind or inner clarity or something external to us that we seek. I have used visualization to heal my own ailments, and I have visualized positive aims on behalf of other people. When I pray for someone who is ill, I picture that person as healthy, doing what he or she loves.

Visualizing an image can bring focus to a desired aim. Sometimes I picture a waterfall when I want to cleanse my spirit. I have also heard of visualizations that clear all of the "cobwebs" from the crevices of one's mind and spirit. For those of us who are visual learners, an image may be the key to channeling our thoughts in a certain direction.

Which image I channel depends on my goal. When I start my day or when I do not have a particular result in mind, I visualize filling myself with blue and white as I breathe, which to me represent peace and love, respectively. I visualize the breath of love starting in the heels of my feet and working upwards through the back of my body, up through the spine, reaching to the crown chakra, continuing to the light of the stars. Then I picture it flowing back down to the front side, through my heart, down my legs to my feet and into the ground. For me, this visualization materializes as a sensation—one that is both enlightening and grounding. I feel lighter as I picture love rising up through my body. I experience grounding as I imagine it flowing downward, through my feet and into the ground, to the center of the earth. I take a few moments to exercise this visualization when I start my day. It not only cleans the slate of my mind with a fresh start, but it is also an image to which I can refer as the challenges of the day arise.

The grounding visualization has become essential to me during times when I perceive the surrounding energies to be chaotic or precarious. When I can, I go out with bare feet and walk on the grass or sand, depending on where I am. This is a great way to ground oneself. There is something about feeling the pull of gravity that manifests in me a sense of calm and steadiness. It humbles me in the presence of the earth's force, and it helps to link my mind with my body in a tangible way, reminding me that it is all connected—my own energies and those of the earth. In this visualization, I stand up straight, trying my best to feel the weight of gravity pull at my feet. I start at my crown and think of it pulling my whole body downward, through my feet, down toward the center of the earth. I rest in this sensation for several minutes. I am always impressed at how greatly the visualization can empower me to insulate my conscious and emotions from any negative energy around me.

Truly, we can conceive of any visualization that speaks to us. Whatever the visualization, it has to convey a message that empowers us throughout the day, week, or year. I have experimented with many before I settled on the ones that I find to be most powerful. Maybe it is a willow tree, one that stands tall and strong, but whose limbs are flexible enough to bend with the wind so as not to snap. One time, after I was diagnosed as having had a heart attack, an adopted family member with a medical background shared the image of an old, live oak tree. She told me not to worry because, although I was experiencing an issue in my trunk, my branches and leaves were still beautiful and healthy. Years later, when I repeated this statement to her, she was surprised. "Did I say that?" she asked. For some reason unknown to us at the time, this was the message she was meant to share, and one I was meant to hear.

Grounding myself through visualization is a way to sustain stability amid tumultuous times, just as any visualization helps me to stay connected to my inner self when the outer world comes at me in unpredictable ways.

Setting the Intention

Once I have my mind at peace and my energies focused, I can gear them toward a desired end.

My biggest mantra in life is to always ***set the intention***. What is the intention? It can be whatever goal or vision I wish to achieve in my day, my year, or my life. The intention can be as simple as the desire to be filled with love, or it can be as advanced as the goal of breaking through hardship.

For me, intention reinforces my inner knowing. I have gotten to the point in my life where I know that whatever or whomever I need will arrive. The intention that I set for myself every day is to sustain this inner knowing, to have faith that it does, and always will, hold true. I realize that everything I could ever want or need is inside of me, nestled somewhere between my consciousness as a human being and my potential for infinite adaptation, evolution, and growth.

I have a mirror in my shower that is a four-fold magnification. Every day, I look at myself in this mirror, and I recite to myself several fundamental intentions. I feel the eyes are the pathways to the soul, and looking in the mirror helps me feel connected on a deep level. The following intentions come from a proclamation written by Ann Marie and Rich Work and can be found in their book, *Proclamations of the Soul (1999).*

Note that I have heard of people interchanging the word *soul* with *spirit*. The important thing is that you choose words representing your inner conscious.

> "I choose to be whole, well, and perfect, in mind, body, and soul.
> I choose to have dominion over my mind, body, and soul.
> I choose to exist in peace, joy, and harmony."

Here, I inhale and then exhale, slowly breathing in and out to connect the words to my mind and spirit. Then I continue the proclamation:

> "I command that all of my energies be aligned, centered, focused, and balanced in divine perfection as my highest harmonic consciousness known as *Jane.*
>
> I ask that whatever is for my highest good will happen."

I finish by once again slowly inhaling and then exhaling to connect my mind, body, and spirit. And finally, I recite:

> "I am that I am."

To me, this last line is powerful because it says, "I am all that is possible." That is, it helps to remind me that I am enough, that I am capable of whatever I choose for myself. I stress the word *choose* in these proclamations because they are an important source of empowerment. What do you *choose* for yourself? You can make the decisions; you can choose how you want your life to go. Perhaps you are choosing love over anger, or faith over fear. There is power in the very act of choosing.

I have shared these proclamations with friends, family, and even children and adolescents. As a guidance counselor, I remember pulling non confident students into the administrative bathroom, which was located close to my office. I would ask them to stand in front of the mirror to recite positive intentions to themselves. I would encourage them to devise their own intentions or choose words or sayings they felt compelled by. They would stand there saying, "I will have a great day;" or "I will feel confident while taking this test;" or "I am confident in my sport." Then I would instruct them to recite the same lines each morning when they got out of bed. Over time, many students benefited from these exercises in intention.

At times, my intentions have been so powerful that they have inadvertently steered me off the course of protocol. Once, when I was working as a guidance counselor, my two colleagues and I were asked to attend a guidance meeting at Pottsgrove High School. We were carpooling, but we didn't have directions. I had just started learning a technique on reading my body's cues using a pendulum. I thought I might try it after we had stopped for breakfast, so I proposed to find the way. My underlying (unconscious) intention, though, was to miss the meeting. Anyone who knew me back then knew that I never liked meetings. "Don't ask me to go," I would say. I never wanted to listen if it didn't pertain to something I deemed valuable. Often, I would try to find a way out. Sure enough, on the Pottsgrove trip, I used my new technique, which I hadn't practiced much yet, and we got lost. We ended up arriving at the school for lunch, having missed the morning meeting. The three of us shared a laugh; we had enjoyed the "trip" I had led us on. I realized later that my intention, which was to miss the meeting, had overpowered everything else.

Another time, a colleague and I ended up in the student union building of the college where we were meant to attend a counselors' meeting. We started talking to the students while shooting pool. We learned a lot from them about the school and its programs. Then, a distinguished man came in and asked if we were part of the guidance group. He informed us it was time for lunch and politely invited us to follow him to the dining hall. When we arrived, the gentleman had my colleague sit at the front table with him. (It was then that we learned he was the president of the college).

When my close friend Roe was hospitalized with a septic intestine, her doctors thought they would lose her. Roe was not aware of what was happening because she was under heavy sedation. When she came to consciousness, she could feel the energy of all of the people praying for her. I went to visit her in the hospital and brought her a candle and an angel ornament. I also gave Roe a stone, which held the vibration "connection to the earth" written on its label.

"Connection to the Earth"

From the Divine Love that flows within my Being.
I proclaim my desire to remain in my physical body so I may experience and fulfill my journey in peace and joy upon the Earth.
I see those energies within me that are connected to Creation. Flowing through my Being, reconnecting with the Earth in Divine Perfection.
And so it is.

From *Proclamations of the Soul* by Rich Work, 1999

I read the proclamation to her that connected with the stone. I asked her if it made sense to her. Roe had taken a Symmetry class that I had taught, so she was aware of how powerful the proclamations could be.

She said yes, and so we recited the proclamation together. Later, she told me how important this stone and its proclamation were to her.

A year later, I had another friend who was very ill. I went back to the gem show to get the same stone for my friend. When I did, one of the owners, Dave, said that he did not remember ever having a stone with that designation—the connection to the earth—on it. He gave me a blank stare when I asked him for that specific one. Somehow, with this exchange, I knew that it would not be helpful to my friend because it was not her time to stay, and I knew she would be passing on.

Something as simple as a stone or an object can help us direct our intentions. It can serve as a reminder or it can empower us in some way. The key is to assign a meaning to it. Roe later told me that the stone helped pull her through the hardship because when she held it in her hand, it triggered a certain energy. We can use these little tools as ways to direct our intentions in a positive way.

I would visit Roe in the hospital and tell her, "I *know* you will get well." I had received this answer in my meditation for her. The repetition of this idea added to all of the support, prayers, and love she was receiving from family and others. Although her fate was uncertain throughout the hardship, Roe's inner resolve, deep faith, and the unwavering love of her family and friends helped her pull through to a full recovery.

The answers to our questions are rarely obvious, and often, they go against our perceptions and others' perceptions of us. Some say that our biggest weaknesses are actually doorways into secret strengths. This is why I find it so critical to look beyond the surface, both in others and in ourselves. You never know what may be lying underneath—whether a hidden passion or unknown strength. In fact, we often go through hardships to realize our inner strengths.

Our dear friends Phil and Maureen are living examples of this perseverance against personal limitations. Phil was one of my students when I was a guidance counselor at Mifflin. In his childhood and into adulthood, he was always a slim person. At age sixty, he shocked many of his friends and family when he decided to become a firefighter. When he brought his firefighter's suit to our house one day, we were struck by how heavy it was; we could hardly pick it up. Not only was he fairly slender, but he was also the oldest trainee in his company. To this day, he is a brave and valiant firefighter serving his community. It was a powerful transformation, and it brought me great joy to watch him come into his own inner knowing time and time again.

Phil's wife Maureen has overcome similar challenges. She is also a smaller, light person, but she carries a big bite. I like traveling to New York City with her, because she's bold and decisive and certainly holds her ground. Through most of her life, Maureen was afraid of water. She grew up in Washington Heights, and because she didn't have many opportunities to be around water, she developed a fear around it. In her adult years, she decided to face up to her fear by learning how to swim.

Maureen has faced challenges where she, too, has had to fight instinctual fear to enter a deeper inner knowing. When her mother was ill and facing her last months in this lifetime, Maureen did not want to let her go. Maureen would visit with her and try to instill hope. "You can pull through this; you *will* get better," she would assure her mother.

As the months passed, we were all there to support Maureen and her mother as they went through the difficult time. And then, one night, her mother came through to me with a message. She told me that she was ready to leave this life, but she would not do so until Maureen could let her go. This is a predicament I see with many families—often, people are not ready to let their loved ones pass, even if the loved one is ready to leave this lifetime.

I contemplated the decision as to whether to tell Maureen about this message I received from her mother. And if so, when and how? Since I had known Phil, her husband, for longer and had a good relationship with him, I felt it was best to share the message with him first. We decided that Phil would share the message with Maureen when he felt it was the right time.

Several months later, I received a phone call from Phil when we were in Las Vegas visiting our son. Phil told me that he finally felt it was the appropriate time to share the special message with Maureen, and so he did. In his phone call to me, he passed the phone to Maureen, and we spoke about it openly. I later learned that Phil's mother and sister had received the same message from Maureen's mother that I had received. When Maureen was able to let her mother go, her mother passed on.

It is not always easy breaking through our fears and limitations, but when we find the courage to do so, we open doors into great healing and empowerment, joy and understanding.

I believe that this concept is critical to not only our emotional and spiritual well-being, but our physical well-being, too. Our perceptions about our health are so powerful—they have the potential to either enchain us, or to set us free. This is especially true of pain, something most people experience in differing degrees at some point in their lives. I developed a trick that helps me alter my perceptions of the chronic pain I have had in my knees for many years. Rather than associate the sensation with pain, I describe it as chatter. People will often hear me say, "My knees are talking to me today."

Our words themselves can trigger fear, which is why I replace *cancer* with *prunie* and *pain* with foreign languages. When we associate these setbacks with something that makes us smile and move on, we can set ourselves up to be released from the pain, rather than get caught up in the fear of it. I greatly value the power of my own thought and its ability to influence my reality. When I think about my body, I try to think as positively as possible. For the most part, I have come out stronger, healthier, and happier from this self-fulfilling prophecy of perception and reality.

The concept of intention may seem abstract at first, but it is a tool worth exploring and understanding. Like a muscle, it must be exercised to develop to its full capacity. When we learn how to use it, it holds inexhaustible potential to impact the changes in our lives we wish to see. In fact, it is a powerful resource I have used to heal my injuries, cure myself of illness, and uncover the answers to my most profound questions.

Whatever end we desire, big or small, we can achieve it through conscious effort. It all starts with setting the intention.

8

Honor the Mystery

Faith is a knowledge within the heart, beyond the reach of proof.
—Kahlil Gibran

One time, I drove my father down a one-way street, going the wrong way. When I saw the cars coming and realized what I had done, I pulled a U-turn in the middle of the road and proceeded directly through a stop sign. My father glared at me with a discerning look.

"Don't worry, Dad. I have my guardian angels with me," I explained. We both shared a strong belief in angels and guides.

"Yes, Jane," he said, "but do you have enough?"

***

One evening, I fell asleep listening to a meditation that was to help me connect to another dimension. I awoke feeling somewhat surprised that nothing had come through for me overnight.

The next day, I received a phone call from my friend Janice, whom I met at college. We have remained close for sixty years.

Janice asked me, "Jane, where were you last night?"

"In my bed," I replied without hesitation. "Never mind where I was last night, Janice. Guess where I am now—at the Fifty-Ninth street beach!" I explained to her that Ted and I were spending the weekend at the shore. I did not fully understand why she was asking me this question.

"No, you weren't," Janice responded. "You were with me in another dimension."

Janice then described a vivid dream she had experienced the night before she called me. It was the same night I had done the meditation. She said that I came to her bed, took her hand, and lifted her up with me as we traveled into the sky. I guided her in a flight through this other dimension, where she said she experienced the most intense sensation she has ever felt.

"It was like the highest sexual climax," Janice said as she explained the experience.

I was not surprised to hear her description. It validated the sensation that my Uncle Bob once shared with my dad as his experience on the other side. While at his retirement home, my dad received a message from Uncle Bob from the other side, who described for my dad the deep unconditional love he was experiencing. He knew he was not going to get my dad's attention by saying simply, "It is great here;" he was smart enough to know that the mention of sex would get him to listen. Uncle Bob described it by saying, "Sex is great over here."

I think it was the best way to explain the profound unconditional love that someone's spirit can experience even when their physical body dies. When we are completely embraced by this feeling of pure, intense, perfect, unconditional love, it is the highest form of pleasure that one can experience.

Afterward, my dad tried to convince the retirement home's chaplain, Mary Ellen, to include this message in her sermon, so all of the "old people" (a category that my father did not belong to, as he saw it) knew what they had to look forward to when they passed on.

***

Once, I walked in the door to my home with the computer blaring the song "What a Wonderful World" by Louis Armstrong, just a few moments after I had been singing the very same song in the car. When I walked over to the computer, I saw that it was not even turned on.

There are moments that make us sit back and say, "Hey, there is something going on here that is beyond what we know." We are learning that we cannot dismiss these mysteries that infuse our world. The magic of life is everywhere, and when we choose to notice it, we can appreciate the marvels that make our earthly experience come to life, while explaining the bigger questions as to why we are here and where we are going.

I believe, one of the sacred gifts of my life are the guardian angels that surround me and protect me through all that I do. There have been times when I have felt their power quite vividly, like the time I hit a dirt mount that sent my car flying into the air. I remember looking out of the window and seeing the ground underneath. I prepared myself for the worst. But suddenly, I felt as though someone picked up the car and slammed it down onto the ground in its upright position. When I opened my eyes, I looked around, and although my arm was dangling from its socket, I was fine, and my car was resting on its four wheels again.

I experienced a similar angelic presence protecting me when my car's brakes went out as I was cruising down a hill. I kept pumping them, but there was no response. I looked ahead and figured I would end up in the field at the bottom of the hill, so at least I knew I wouldn't injure anyone. But shockingly, when I reached the corner at the bottom of the hill, my brakes kicked in. The moment represented one of several times that I truly felt the power of something that was not of this earth—a sort of angelic presence protecting me. Since I always felt my angel had to be really big and strong, I adopted Archangel Michael. I know my dad would agree with this selection, as he knew how I would get myself into all sorts of predicaments. I could not count the number of times he asked me (about my angels), "But, Jane, do you have enough?"

When I was visiting Canyon de Chelly National Monument with Ted, his brother Bruce and his late wife Betty, I experienced a profound sense of connection to another dimension. Instead of using the "shake and bake" trucks, as they are called, to travel through the canyon, we hired a private Jeep with a native Navajo guide. As we were riding through the canyon, I was truly overcome by its majestic beauty and meaning. I felt a deep sensation come over me. While we were riding, I started hearing a song, softly at first, and then it grew louder in my ears. Tears began pouring down my face, as they always do when I am struck with profound meaning or spiritual connection. I told our guide that I was hearing a song, and suddenly, he began singing the same exact melody out loud.

"Is this it?" he asked.

"Yes," I replied, struck with emotion. "What is it?" I asked him.

He told me that it represented the music of healing sung by the ancients. Could he have been referring to the Anasazi? They were rumored to have lived in the canyon first. I have tried many times to find this music..but to no avail.

This moment carried special meaning for me because it occurred shortly after I discovered the breast lump. Ted was the only person who knew about it at the time. The experience in Canyon de Chelly was one of the first signs I received that I would be all right.

Sometimes, these signs are there to guide me on my own journey, while other times, messages have come through only to verify what someone else is feeling.

When my neighbor's wife passed away, he was stricken with grief, as anyone would be. Later, as he was preparing to move away, he took Ted and I out to dinner as a farewell. When we dropped him off at his home and said good-bye, I watched him slowly walk up his driveway, and then, I noticed that his wife was walking by his side with her hand on his shoulder. They were surrounded by their beloved dogs, who had also passed on. A message came through to me from his departed wife that was meant for him. Tears poured down my face as I was struck with the beautiful scene and her message.

I wanted to share what I saw in this profound moment with my neighbor, but we had not discussed spiritual things, so I was not exactly sure how to approach him. Yet, I wanted him to know that I saw his wife with him, and I wanted to share her message intended just for him. So, I decided to write him a letter and mail it to him at his new home.

When I did not hear back from him for several days, I thought that my letter may not have had the same feeling for him as it did for me. I was just happy to have shared the moment with him. But then, a week later, he called me.

He said to me, simply, "That night, I felt her beside me, too."

It was not the only time that I experienced someone else's energy in a profound way. In January of 1993, after recently retiring from my career in education, I went to an elder hostel with my friend Ruth. The hostel was at Edgar Cayce's retreat center in Virginia Beach. Since I was a young child, I had admired Edgar Cayce for his emphasis on this magical facet of humanity—all of the connections that we cannot explain, fueled by mysterious vibrations and energies. The hostel had us doing various exercises in groups of people. I partnered up with a woman from York, whom I had met at the retreat and who became a treasured friend. For one of the exercises, we were asked to place our hands on each other's shoulders. When I placed my hands on her shoulders, tears immediately started pouring down my face, and I suddenly felt intense anguish.

"What do you feel?" my partner asked me.

I explained to her the sensations I was experiencing in that moment.

Then, with an expression of understanding, she explained. "What you experienced was my grief from losing my son to suicide several years ago," she said.

It struck me that, if these feelings were still on her body's surface for me to detect and feel, they must not be truly healed yet. I wondered if such a loss could ever truly be healed. A loss as big as the one she had experienced can remain with a person for a long time, if not forever. It made me think about the things that get trapped in our energy fields— emotions, feelings, sensations, experiences, and memories—things that, when unattended, can turn into huge burdens for us to bear. They can manifest in many different forms, such as physical ailment, chronic pain, mental illness, emotional trauma, intense fear, and many other forms. While there are no right or wrong ways to grieve, the key to truly *healing* many of these problems is to pinpoint the emotional or *non*physical source of the ailment, and to try to heal that component first. How we choose to live is what is important.

There was another time when I was feeling someone's energy field at a similar healing workshop, and I was struck by the contrast in temperature of the person's body. Half of his body was cold, and half was hot. When I shared this experience with him, he did not share any explanation. Later, at the end of the retreat, when I suppose he was feeling safe to share, he said to me, "I want to tell you what you felt."

"Okay," I said openly.

"I'm bipolar," he said.

This concept of nonphysical self-healing is embraced by the Healing Codes, a set of healing techniques developed by Dr. Loyd, who was searching for medical answers. Dr. Ben Johnson also joined his research efforts, and together they promoted what Dr. Loyd developed as the Healing Codes. Dr. Johnson was able to cure himself of ALS, and to this day, they offer the program to ALS patients for free. (Loyd and Johnson, *The Healing Codes*, 2004-2006).

In the technique, the first step to healing any physical ailment begins with self-forgiveness. I learned not to accept guilt in my life, and I believe that has been very helpful to my healing process. The one time I did experience guilt was as a child, when I felt pressured to exclude one of my classmates from my birthday party because she was marginalized in the class due to her head lice. I suppose I was more worried about pleasing the other girls in the class than I was concerned about acting honestly and truthfully to myself. It was one of the few moments in my life where I felt I strayed from my own conscious, choosing to act in a way that was highly influenced by others.

It was not until years later that I realized I had never forgiven myself for this act of exclusion. True to the Healing Codes, I had to enact self-forgiveness before I could truly heal and move on from it.

There is so much we cannot explain, and when we are open to the phenomena of life, we give ourselves a chance to experience intense clarity, connection, and love. We may not always be able to explain it, but that does not mean the magic isn't there for a reason. It often unlocks important clues for us in our life's journey or acts as a sign to help us make a decision or set us on a certain new path. We must let go of the idea that everything must be assigned a factual connection, and rather, honor the gifts we are given that are not based on facts, but rather, on energy, on vibration, and on unconditional love.

***

When my father developed Parkinson's in his late seventies, his doctor put him on all sorts of medications. His body, like mine, was sensitive to drugs. I knew there were too many medications in his body. He seemed like a zombie to me. When his best friend passed away, my dad's emotional sensitivity augmented his illness. I disliked all of his medications—especially when I learned of all the side effects. When his doctor doubled his medications, my dad went into convulsions.

He was taken to the Graduate Hospital in Philadelphia since I had already made arrangements for him to see a doctor there. I knew they were doing innovative things with the research and treatment of Parkinson's. The doctor there immediately took my father off of each and every one of his medications. Thankfully, my dad listened—because the doctor was Irish. My brother and I helped him in the days that followed his return from the hospital as he underwent the withdrawal symptoms.

My dad had a strong will. Despite his sensitivities, he never wanted to explain to his heart specialist and other physicians why it was that he could not take certain medications. He would simply sit in the doctor's office with his eyes shut, a big smile on his face. I was the one who always had to explain. After one of the visits, I asked my dad why he wouldn't just open up and explain to his physicians that he had a history with certain drugs, and that he preferred to follow the course of treatment that the Graduate Hospital had advised him on.

"It's way more fun watching you try to explain," he laughed.

My dad went to a retirement center when he began needing additional help with his routine and when my mom developed Alzheimer's. He filled this experience with stories that caused laughter, tears, and almost always, trouble. It was like him to stir the pot. His intention was to have fun, to enjoy every moment of life until the day he died. In his last several years, his health began deteriorating. The way I see it, he chose to go into a coma when he felt it was enough. Everything in life was on his terms. I inherited my will from him.

One evening, I was sitting at my dad's bedside. He told me that in his room was a big angel, and that his deceased family and friends were there with him, too. It was the first time that everyone was there at the same time in that room. While it was a normal occurrence for my dad to have conversations with departed loved ones, the fact that all of them were there along with a big angel would have normally been a sign to me that he was leaving. But I was focused on taking my future daughter-in-law to Hershey for her birthday, so the sign slipped past me. I said good night and let him rest.

The very next day, he fell into a coma. It was December 3, 1996. I went to see him at the home. The doctors advised me that he would not last long, that he was slipping fast.

When I drove home after the visit that day, my dad came through to me with a clairvoyant message of intricate detail. I pulled to the side of the road, stopped the car, and listened.

He told me that he would not pass on while my brother and I were in the room. He also told me that he wanted his graveside service and wake to be held the Friday before Christmas, because that's when his friends would be free and family members would be home from Florida. Then, he went on to discuss the food and drink menu, which would feature beer and wine, but not whiskey. Finally, my dad told me not to worry about the weather. The sun would be shining and there would be a wind at our backs, he assured me, just as the old Irish blessing confers.

When I got home, I wanted to follow through on his requests. I found it unusual that he would specifically choose to omit whiskey from the drink menu at his wake, as his Irish upbringing would predict the opposite. But when I phoned the Port of Call in Ocean City where the wake would be held, I was reminded that Ocean City was a dry town at the time, and that the venue would only be permitted to serve beer and wine. I was stunned—my dad's message was suddenly validated in my mind.

Next, I called the funeral director to find out how long he could hold my dad's body because we were looking at a December 20 wake (per my dad's request), and it was only December 3. The director responded that he could hold the body for ten days. It's in that moment that I knew my dad would not be leaving us until December 10 so that his graveside service could be on the day he wanted. Without a doubt in my mind, I proceeded to set up the arrangements for December 20. I often wondered later what the funeral director thought about my odd question.

As sure as anything, my dad passed away at a moment when my brother and I had left his room to go to the cafeteria to have lunch. We returned to the sight of the nurses crying outside of my dad's room.

I turned to my brother and asked him for the date, to which he replied, December 10.

It was December 19, the day before the burial service. The weather was horrific. It was the first day of a three-day nor'easter headed for the shore. Everyone was nervous because my dad had specifically requested the outdoor graveside service. But I reassured everyone: "Don't worry. There might be a wind, but the sun will be shining."

The next day, we went to the graveside. Without my knowledge, the chairs had been set up to face the sun, which was shining bright that day in Ocean City. Our friends and family trickled in, and as we all began to take our seats, we felt the wind at our backs. The words of the Old Irish Blessing were loud and clear within all our hearts:

> *May the road rise to meet you.*
> *May the wind be always at your back.*
> *May the sun shine warm upon your face.*

May the rain fall soft upon your fields.
Until we meet again, may God hold you in the palm of
his hand.

As human beings, we are made of mind, body, and spirit. But the sum of the parts is greater than the whole. When our physical body dies, the culmination of our consciousness and our spirit remains. People—including myself—have been known to communicate with people in comas or with the deceased for this very reason. I believe these communications exist to deliver important knowledge from one realm to the next. Someone who may be retiring her physical body may feel there is a message she wants to deliver to her loved ones, and often, this information is vital to shaping the life path of those around her. The meanings carried in these messages may help someone forgive himself in order to move on, or they may shed light on the reasons why we have been brought to this point at all.

Healers have told me that I have "clear seeing," and perhaps some people are more inclined than others to communicate in this way. But I feel that we must all be open to the possibility of tapping into someone's spirit or consciousness even after they are gone. It is not out of the question for any of us. Many believe that, often, the best time to try to connect or meditate with someone spiritually is to choose a day that was special to both of you.

There are many ways by which two people can communicate: one is through words; another is possible when two conscious minds can connect, even without a physical presence. We could call it a metaphysical connection, in a sense. Often, this knowledge is transmitted through signs or life lessons, and when we are open to perceiving them, we unlock larger pieces of the puzzle for our lives and others.

***

Years after my dad passed, I received a message from him on July 4. Ted and I always get together with a group of golfers and their spouses over the holiday. I had just gotten off of the phone with my brother to wish him an early Orangeman's day, which was July 12. Our guests were coming through the front door when my dad came through with his message.

He said, "Get on the phone, and call your brother. He has to know this."

My father went on to explain that my brother should be relieved of his guilt. My brother had developed type-1 diabetes as an adult. My parents worried that he felt responsible for passing it onto his daughter, Corinne, who was diagnosed with juvenile diabetes. My father came through with this message to explain that, in fact, my brother was meant to have diabetes so that he could prepare his family for what was to come—which was childhood diabetes in his daughter. My father said that my brother had taken on this disease out of his soul's great love for his daughter.

As the message was coming through and my father was insisting that I call my brother with the information, I responded, "Not now, dad. I just got off the phone with Tommy. I will call him tonight."

But my father insisted. "No, you are to call him right now."

So I did. I called my brother and gave him our dad's message. I explained that I had to call him at this time. I explained that our dad was insisting. Because of my father's pleading, there was no question in my mind that this was important to share with him at this specific time.

When I shared the message with my brother, his first reaction was, "What's this about? I don't feel guilt over this."

Incidentally, a couple of days later, my brother called me and told me that his daughter, Corinne, was taken to the hospital after she had a diabetic incident on the same day that I had called Tommy, July 4.

In that moment, I understood why my father had insisted that I call my brother so urgently. Later, I would write a letter to my brother, explaining to him the special connection I had with my dad and the reason why I had called him so pressingly on that fateful day. Later, I found the letter and learned from Tommy that I had never actually sent it to him.

It's hard to explain the spiritual connection that Dad and I had. We seemed to know each other's thoughts without talking. In the last six years, I have had a lot of experiences where I will receive messages that come through and have been able to prepare families and help them through difficult times.

I am trying to explain, Tom, that this is nothing I have asked for—it just happens. The morning after Thanksgiving, the year Dad passed, I was awoken early in the morning. Usually, I don't look at the clock, but for some reason, I did. The time reflected my lucky numbers. I felt Dad's presence in the room. He was laughing and remembering all the things we had done together and ended up reminding me of the time I drove down a one-way street with him in the wrong direction. "Don't worry, Dad, I have my guardian angels with me," I said. "Yes, but do you have enough?" he asked, laughing.

I had the sense he wanted me to remember what I had told him. With that, I felt his spirit leave the room and I woke Ted up. I told Ted what had happened, and I felt Dad was leaving. I ran to the nursing home, only to find him in good spirits and laughing and telling me of the two big angels that had been with him in his room. The next couple of days with him were the same. The day before he went into his coma, he seemed tired, but I truly didn't have an idea that he was going to be in a comatose state the very next day. The only hint I had was that he told me all of the angels plus Uncle John, Uncle Bob, and others were in the room with him.

I was told by an old minister once that I had "clear seeing," and that I could use it to help others.

Dad said to me, "What day is this, Jane?" It was July 4, Independence Day. "Time for Tom to be free of guilt."

Years later, Corinne and her husband Curt would witness the birth of their daughter Caden Jane on July 4.

There was another instance when I felt an urgency to call my brother's home at a particular moment, and again, it was the timing that ended up being helpful in a way I did not understand until later. When my mother passed away, Cornwall Manor called me with the news. It was in the middle of the night, and I wanted to inform my brother, but I also contemplated waiting until early morning so as not to disturb him in his sleep. But when I thought more about it, I recalled that my brother had insisted that I call him with the update—*no matter what hour it may be*. When I picked up the phone to call him, I reached his wife Peggy. It was fateful that I happened to call their home in that moment, because my call had awoken Peggy to her husband having a diabetic episode. Thankfully, she was able to help him through it. It was the gift that my mom had sent for my brother from the other side.

***

I truly do not believe that I have anything special. I have never had an ability to reach people on the other side; it is others who have come to me with messages. I believe that if we are open to receiving these messages or, more simply, perceiving the signs, we can gain a better understanding of why things happen, and we can begin to answer larger questions about the circumstances and events of our lives and our world.

These metaphysical connections are not limited to people; they can also occur between animals, plants, anything or anyone in the natural world. *The Celestine Prophecy* and *The Secret Life of Plants* and other books have explored the way plants respond to human intention in a positive way from both a metaphysical and scientific perspective. And there is no doubt that many of us have established ways of communicating with animals.

One of the most unusual messages I received occurred when I was getting a massage. I sat up and held the hand of my massage therapist, Jane G., who has since become a close friend of mine. I held her hand while tears streamed down my face. The therapist's dog, Sox, came to me during the session and wanted me to tell her that he would be leaving soon, that it was time for him to leave, and that he loved her and wanted her to know it was his decision to leave. He hoped that this information could help her understand the decision she needed to make in the long-term relationship she felt she needed to end with her partner.

At the time of receiving the message, I had no knowledge of Sox, let alone his illness, and I did not understand the information that was coming to me. But when I shared the message with Jane, it registered with her immediately. She told me the story. She and her then-partner had gotten Sox as a puppy ten years before. She was in the process of leaving her partner, but she couldn't bear to leave Sox. Neither one wanted to give up the dog. When I shared Sox's message with her, it became clear to her that Sox was choosing to leave this life in order to release her from the relationship. Out of his great love for her, he helped make her decision easier.

The evening before Sox passed away, my friend, her boyfriend, and Sox slept on the floor together, and then they shared a breakfast of bacon. The next day, he died in her arms. Rather than feeling sorrow, she was able to experience great love and joy. His passing and the meaning of it unlocked an important piece of the puzzle for my friend. She later said, "Rather than closing down to the pain, we must be open to the beauty."

I find it is so important to be open to these streams of consciousness that come through to us in whatever form. I, like my father, have often been able to communicate with people from other realms. I know when someone from another realm is coming through to me with a message because tears begin immediately start pouring down my face. I usually have to go to a quiet place to meditate and receive the message. In this way, I have been able to receive knowledge and pieces of information from people in comas and the deceased, and it has served to help their families and friends.

My favorite Proclamation!

"Desires of My Heart"

From the Divine Love that flows within my Being
I ask that my Being be filled with Infinite Love, Infinite Healing,

Infinite Protection, Infinite Power and Wisdom.
I call forth my Grand Adventure in feelings and emotions
that will bring me Happiness and Joy.
And so it is.

From *Proclamations of the Soul* by Rich Work, 1999

9

We Are All One

There are no facts, only interpretations.
- Friedrich Nietzsche

I once encountered a man who had given up on his faith. I met him in the waiting room of the oncology center at Fox Chase, where Ted was getting his radiation treatment for prostate cancer. While Ted was in the treatment room, I struck up a conversation with the man sitting next to me. He looked ashen-gray and seemed to be filled with sorrow. I learned he was there for the same treatments as Ted. The man told me that he could no longer believe in his Jewish faith or in God. He said that, after being married for more than fifty years, he and his wife were just beginning to get along when she died.

"How could I believe in anything anymore?" he asked.

Considering the illness he was facing, I wanted to help bring his hope back to life. We started having deeper conversations over coffee and hot chocolate. I shared some of my struggles and lessons with him. He started opening up. Soon, we were exchanging stories and laughing. His facial expressions and body language started changing. I sensed that slowly, hope seeped back into his being.

We kept in touch following the treatment sessions, as many of us did after meeting at Fox Chase. We would have regular lunch dates to keep up with each other's lives. Once, when I called him to schedule a lunch date, he joked that he was too busy to meet because his new girlfriend was consuming his time. Joy and laughter infused his life once again. His prognosis had been poor, but in whatever time he had remaining, he was able to rediscover happiness.

***

When I first started encountering health problems, I was hesitant to share the stories of my struggles with others. Even though I maintained close relationships with my friends through the various tests in my life, I tended to feel as though the trials were mine to overcome, and I did not want to attract pity, sympathy or—most importantly—negative thoughts. I tried to reassure myself that whomever or whatever I would need in my life would eventually arrive. It was an inner knowing I had carried with me since the age of twelve.

It did not take long for me to see that I was not alone. Former students, friends, and friends-of-friends called to talk. Sometimes they sought answers; other times, they wanted nothing but to be heard by a nonjudgmental ear. Often, people merely wanted to hear my story and learn from its lessons. Indeed, we must heal our own wounds, but we can ask a friend for a bandage. One must realize the power of his or her inner knowing, but there are people and events that serve as the sounding board for that knowledge. We may share stories to learn of other options, or identify certain patterns, or feel connected in the parallels. Sometimes, there is strength in discovering that the world of possibilities for healing is as infinite as the stars in the sky.

As new tests of adversity arose among the people in my life, I had a revelation. We each carry a unique piece to the puzzle. I think of my two close friends, Roe and Theresa, and how the three of us were each challenged with life-threatening illness; we each faced grim prognoses, and we each overcame the hardship in our own distinct ways. We are separated by three unique faiths—Protestantism, Catholicism, and a Buddhist/Quaker-like spirituality—and three different healing paradigms. Our respective faiths liberated us from the illness, and we were each fortunate to overcome them. The stories were the same, with only the names, illnesses, and faiths changed around.

The struggles that shape us and teach us are the same ones that we are meant to share, so that we may piece together the ultimate puzzle of our universe. Often, sharing our stories means exposing aspects of ourselves that we prefer to conceal—whether it be fear or insecurity, pain or weakness. But all of human vulnerability is universal. In the challenge lies the key to progress. The stories serve as points on a graph. When we step back from it, we can detect the patterns.

Why are we here, on this planet, living these stories?

What are the lessons we are meant to share that will enable us to evolve?

How can we shape where we are going?

What a shame it would be, to see only the morsels of our own stories, while the masterpiece of the entire portrait existed at our fingertips.

***

If our struggles and their lessons endow us with the pieces of the puzzle, it is our ability to connect that will enable us to assemble the pieces. Faith is unique to each individual, but the lessons we derive from it are—more often than not—universal. When we bother to look beneath the surface of the boundaries, divisions, and pretenses, we can uncover the threads that tie us all together as a human race.

"I am led to give this to you," said my son's friend, Al. "I know you are not Catholic, and I am of Jewish faith. I know you are not religious. But your son has told me that you are spiritual."

I accepted the small box from his hands and opened it. To my surprise, it was a set of rosary beads. They were a brilliant blue color.

"Oh, look, Jane," remarked Ted, who was standing with me as I opened the gift, "they are your color. Blue, for peace."

Several days later, I woke up and felt the desire to look again at the box that had contained the beads. I saw the image of a woman holding roses. When I flipped the box over, I discovered a prayer, that of Saint Theresa. Although I am not Catholic, this carried meaning for me, as I had received several verifications in my life that one of my guardian angels is a woman holding roses. Later that evening, when I researched Saint Theresa on the Internet, I learned that she had a Jewish grandfather. There, again, was a thread that connected me to this object and the person who had given it to me.

The unusual gift of the rosary from a Jewish friend, the verification of my guardian angel, the blue color standing for peace—this simple exchange deepened my understanding of universal faith. A particular religion or spirituality may enlighten one's path for answers, but the biggest questions for humanity can only be answered when those lessons are shared across divisions. It is amazing, the extent to which the religions of the world share so many of the same foundational teachings. When we release judgment and focus on what unites us, we can begin to benefit from the lessons.

I have learned to gain my strength and compassion not from any single religion, but from the teachings of many faiths and philosophies. Whenever I receive a sign like this, I feel that my faith in the universe is deepened. These guideposts help lead the way when I am lost, or verify that I am meant to pursue the path I am walking.

As a child, I was always asking myself, "How much of our lives are predestined?" I grew up going to a Presbyterian church, whose guiding pillar is predestination. I did not understand why we had to be good and truthful if the universe had already determined our fate. Later in life, I would come to answer this question for myself. I now believe that we enter into this earth plane with some kind of a script—things we are meant to accomplish, learn, clear, understand, aspire to. If it doesn't happen in this lifetime, then it will in others. Past lives and even parallel lives determine much of our current life. How much of these aspects we understand and overcome is up to us. We can shape the patterns.

Over the years, I have formed a spirituality of my own creation with lessons of various faiths mixed in. When someone asks for my religion,

I answer that I'm one-third Quaker, one-third Buddhist, and one-third Unity. No dogma. Dogma restricts. That's my fixture.

My triad of spirituality includes Quaker because it taught me tolerance for all and to quietly reflect on one's inner light. I align with Buddhism for its belief in meditation and inner peace. And I value Unity for of its positivity and recognition of the power of thought. Unity Church services often end with the song, "Let There Be Peace on Earth, and Let It Begin with Me." That is a mantra I have carried with me through my life.

Of course, I do not limit myself to certain forms of worship. I draw lessons from religious texts ranging from the Bible to the Koran, from prophets, philosophers, shamans, religious leaders and healers, from friends and strangers, even from YouTube videos and Facebook posts. Everything in front of us is meant to be our teacher; there are lessons to be learned from the most banal moments to the most inspiring events. Finding one's own spirituality sometimes means adapting different aspects of faith to one's own identity. The highest spirituality resides within us.

Most importantly, at the foundation of my spirituality is an *inner knowing*. There is a paramount difference between believing and knowing, and the concept of knowing is not just a certainty of the mind. To me, it is a higher state of consciousness. It is a knowledge beyond the scope of "belief" that rests somewhere in our soul. It expresses itself in many ways, often the simplest being our intuition. The notion is a pillar of many religions. For some, it may mean that God's hand will always guide us in the direction He has intended for us. For me, it is a knowing that whatever is in my highest good will happen, even if it is not what I thought I wanted or needed at the time.

To break through hardship, we may leverage our individual faiths or whatever spiritual or physical means we choose, but the most important lesson for me has been to sustain this *inner knowing* that there is a higher reason for everything. And if I choose to learn what it is, I can grow in unprecedented ways.

Like so many others, my life has not been easy. Yet my feeling is one of deep gratitude. I acknowledge that the hardships have translated into my greatest strengths; with each challenge comes an opportunity to learn, grow, build character, dig deeper, and discover the curing effect of love. When we step back from the struggle, it is easier to understand the bigger reason. My two greatest gifts in life were also two of my most painful events: my adolescent depression and being diagnosed with terminal cancer.

There are many times when one's *inner knowing* will be tested. Pain, stress, trauma, and difficulty arise in our lives many times over. Tragedy occurs. And often, the picture of our world rears its ugly head. It may be difficult to remind oneself that "these things happen for a reason." But when we choose to sustain that inner knowing, we are prompted to *look* for the reason. Often, these events present us with an opportunity to look at an issue in a different light or set us on a path to change things. We can either view them as tragedies and fill ourselves with pity and remorse, or we can see them as little keys—keys that will unlock new doors for humanity and set us on entirely new paths.

And just as importantly, I look for the signs that serve as verifications for my inner knowing. If we are perceptive and open, the signs always appear. Remember that doubt tends to come from the mind, where our inner knowing comes from the soul.

***

Michael was one of my students at Governor Mifflin. He was acting out in school, and I wanted to get a deeper understanding of why he was behaving in this way. What I learned from him was that the path that he felt he was destined to be on was being blocked. He was experiencing seizures, which prevented him from achieving his lifelong dream of joining the navy. Naturally, he was frustrated, and he channeled those feelings into a sort of rebellion at school: he dared to push the limits, perhaps because he did not feel like he had anything to lose.

I remember telling Michael, "You're on the edge, Mike. Be careful," I would caution him.

He once came to see me in the guidance office with an interesting look on his face. He confided that a friend and he had been fooling around and had just broken one of the school's large windows outside of the gym.

While I was touched that he would confide in me, I did not give him a free pass. I had him look at his options and what the results of those actions would be.

"I think you better fess up," I advised him. "It's the safest thing to do."

Hesitantly, he went into the principal's office to take the blame for his part in the broken window. Later in the day, he came back to my office.

"Honesty doesn't pay," he said to me as he explained. "They're making us pay for the whole window!" (To this day, he remembers exactly the amount he paid for the window, down to the last cent).

We shared a laugh over it at the time, but the lesson was still there. It is so important to walk in someone's shoes before making a judgment. It's not about giving someone a free pass; it's about looking deeper. This was a young man who had lost his dream. Inside, he was angry, so he pushed the limits. When he broke the window, he chose to confess it to me, perhaps to see how far my faith in him would stretch. I only encouraged him to act in his highest self-interest. This was my philosophy as a counselor: I was not meant to clear the door for others, but to empower them to walk through it themselves.

Michael's story demonstrates the importance of abstaining from judgment about someone, especially when we do not know what has happened in someone's life that may bring about their actions or behavior. When I reconnected with him while writing this book, he wished to share these words:

> "The world was waiting for me and I was doing what many teens do, getting ready to fulfill my dream of serving our country, as did my father before me. Then I fell down and had my first seizure. The navy would have nothing to do with me. Not only that, but the Pennsylvania Department of Transportation had a 2-year 'seizure-free' rule before driving a car. Two

weeks before my 16th birthday, my life's dreams became nightmares. I got angry and rebellious. It seemed like the world had it in for me.

Then, I met Jane, my high school counselor. She rescued me from myself. She could see right through my act. The odd thing was that I was glad she could. She was a 'wise friend' who actually cared about my situation, and she was the only one that I felt safe talking to.

Many years later, after the suicide of my father and then my son, I began having frequent thoughts of suicide. If I couldn't follow them in the navy, maybe I should follow them in death. I became afraid and unsure. I needed help. I knew I was broken, but I didn't know how to fix it. Only one wise friend came to mind: Jane. I wondered if she still had that unique ability that she had back in school.

She did.

And I am still here, 65 years old and counting."

***

If we could look into each other's hearts and understand the unique challenges each of us faces, I think we would treat each other much more gently, with more love, patience, tolerance, and care.
—Marvin J. Ashton

***

I had a student at Governor Mifflin who was smart and dedicated to his academics and a shining star on the basketball court. But there was something else, another connection I felt with him that I could not explain, and I would not be able to understand until later in life.

Like with many of my students, we keep in touch to this day. He went on to play basketball at Penn State, and then he played professionally in

Europe for several years. In the late '80s, he and his wife moved back to the United States to raise a family.

He called me when his daughter Katie was battling autoimmune hepatitis, a chronic acute liver disease, at a young age. After spending many frustrating years filtering in and out of hospitals with no successful solutions to the disease, he called me. He knew of my spirituality and affinity to alternative healing, and he thought I might be able to help where conventional medicine was failing. They were able to connect with Dr. Carrie, who worked with her for about a year. It was when Dr. Carrie was away on a vacation that Katie had a relapse and went to the Children's Hospital of Philadelphia (CHOP).

I was in Denver for a meditation retreat, eating lunch at a restaurant with friends, when I received my first message from Katie. At the time, Katie was hospitalized at CHOP and was coming to the end of her battle. As Katie's spirit came through to me, tears started pouring down my face, and I immediately interrupted lunch. The tears had always been a sign that I was to receive a message from someone on the other side. I asked my friends to take me to a quiet place, closed my eyes, and went into a meditation to receive Katie's message. The message was that Katie was not sure if she wanted to stay or leave this life. She had not yet made up her mind.

Over the course of the retreat, it was Katie who consumed my meditations. I received a series of messages from her throughout the week as Katie remained in the hospital in critical condition, struggling with the decision to stay or leave.

Finally, Katie's decision came through to me: if CHOP was going to recommend a liver transplant for her, then Katie would be leaving this earth. She had experienced immense trauma in a past life and did not want to go through it again in this lifetime. The decision was hers.

When her doctors recommended the liver transplant, Katie's course of action was clear to her: she was going to leave in peace. She shared this decision with me in another message. I struggled with this information, as I did not know whether to share it with Katie's parents at the time. I asked for a sign. *Should I tell them?* I asked myself.

111

I called the hospital to reach Katie's parents and check in on her, and it was in that moment that I received my answer. Before I called, I had set a special intention: if I had truly connected with Katie 's wishes, I would be given a sign. The sign would be that if I reached Katie's mother on the phone, then I was meant to withhold the information. If I reached her father, then I was to share the message and Katie's decision.

I phoned the general hospital line, not knowing which room Katie was in. As it rang, I expected to connect to the switchboard. To my surprise, I reached the exact room in which Katie's father had been resting. "Hello? Jane? How did you know which room I was in?" he asked, perplexed. "I have told no one."

Then, he broke the news to me that Katie's doctors were recommending a liver transplant. It was with these verifications that I knew I was meant to share Katie's message with her parents. And I did. They were to know that the decision was Katie's, and that she would purposefully refuse her body's healing so that she would not have to go through with the operation. Katie did not want her parents to blame themselves.

As the days passed, Katie remained in critical care as her doctors waited for her vital signs to improve so she would be well enough for the operation. But it was an operation she did not want; she had made up her decision, and so, she refused to get well.

In Katie's last days, another message came through to me: she wanted her dad to pick up her siblings and bring them to the Philadelphia Zoo. Katie was an animal lover, and she would be there, sharing in their joy.

When I called the hospital again to deliver this message to her parents, Katie's mom answered the phone. She was taken aback and immediately asked how I knew that her husband had picked up the kids and taken them to the zoo, where they were in that exact moment.

As true as the messages she had delivered to me, Katie passed away on March 11, 1998. Her vital signs never improved enough for the transplant. But it wouldn't have mattered. The transplant was not meant for her—she hadn't wanted it. She chose to depart in peace.

It was critical for me to perceive these signs and understand Katie's unspoken intentions through her illness. She had wanted to go in peace, so when the time came for a transplant, she chose to refuse it in her own way. I shared this understanding with her parents so that they would not blame themselves for Katie's outcome. Although it was a difficult outcome to embrace, the silver lining was the fact that Katie had made her own decisions based on the fate that was written into her life script.

When any of us receive these verifications, signs, messages, or any glimpses into the reasons behind the events of our universe, we cannot negate them. The more perceptive we can be as to these clues, the better we can understand the higher reason behind these struggles.

***

We often ask, "Why must tragic things happen in the first place?"

If we look at many of the tragic events in our world, we can find a higher purpose behind them. Unless we examine the roots of violence, we will not be able to stanch its spread. Unless we taper our aggravation of nature, storms will only build stronger and cause more hardship for those affected. Unless we show compassion for all living things, the animals we eat and the plants that nourish us, we will face health problems related to our diets. Illness, both mental and physical, cannot be overcome unless we learn to love and forgive the self.

When twenty-year-old Adam Lanza walked into Sandy Hook Elementary School in Newtown, Connecticut one morning and fatally shot twenty children and six adults, the country grasped for answers. As a nation, we were overcome by sorrow, fear, and despair. I grieved and I mourned for the loss of the children's lives, but I also grieved for Adam Lanza. How sad it was to see a young man so troubled and without any help to turn to. I decided, rather than sending anger, to send love, empathy, and compassion toward him, his family and toward the grieving families. I turned my feelings of sorrow into feelings of hope for humanity. Maybe this, along with so many similar tragedies, will promote more research and help for those dealing with mental illness.

Through our local Spirit on Tap, I heard how the Amish community came together to help the grieving family of the young man who murdered Amish children. I tapped into my knowing that whatever is in society's highest good will happen, and it caused me to view the tragedy in a new light. The shootings reminded all of us how much violence we have in the world. It reminded us that these assault weapons are pervasive, and they are too easily procured. But my biggest question was: Why aren't we dedicating our energy and resources to the root causes of these tragedies—not only to gun control but to mental illness? Just as illness can bring about a change for the better in an individual, so can these senseless acts of violence bring about changes for the common good.

We so often think we are above these injustices, but if we truly look at ourselves, are we the change we wish to see in the world? Are we living truthfully, compassionately toward others? Even ourselves?

In the aftermath of the events of September 11, 2001, I called several of my close friends together to meditate for peace. Before long, a group of seven was joining together every month to pray for peace and justice in the world. Our focus is to send vibrations of peace and love throughout the world, to all the leaders, and to all of their people. The meetings, which have continued through the years, always include a meditation for peace, for understanding, and for compassion throughout our world. Over the years, we have developed a deep bond and share our stories openly. Linda named the group STARS, which stands for Sisters Taking a Risk Spiritually. The group knows that the biggest change we want to see in our world must first occur in ourselves. Finding inner peace and then emanating that energy outward toward our world is the solution over cynicism, anger, or frustration.

The world's problems seem unconquerable, but when we turn to our internal problems and cure ourselves first, that is a powerful shift already. What affects us is also what we, in turn, want to go back and change about the world. If I hadn't gone through the different struggles in my life, I would not have become what I am. The focus of my career was to help the quieter, troubled kids because I felt I could empathize with their problems. I often think, *If I hadn't gone through the depression myself, would I have chosen this path?* My friend Billy was the catalyst and my own journey provided the focus. It all happens for a reason bigger than we may sometimes understand. These events are part of who we are and shape the way we engage with the world going forward.

> *Hold within your hearts the vision for the world you want for yourselves, your families, and for all the people of the earth—a world where peace and love replace war, fear and hatred. Where governments are just, prudent and spiritual. Where there is a fair distribution of all resources, where universal truths live within each heart.*
> —Rich and Ann Marie Work

***

Just as quickly as violence can spread, so can compassion, kindness, and honesty. I believe that compassion is stronger than violence. Love is stronger than fear. I choose to send love and nurturing to those around me. It becomes a reflex rather than a conscious effort.

The universe delivers lessons in peculiar ways. Often, they are painful, frightening, and tragic. But they also jolt our energies and set them on a new path.

> *All truth is truth, but not all truth is* your *truth.*
> —Rich Work

> *Go inside, and awaken your own search for your truth, whatever that may be.*

> *It is time.*

Epilogue
by Stefanie

This is my simple religion
There is no need for temples, no need for complicated philosophy.
Our own brain, our own heart is our temple.
The philosophy is kindness.
Dalai Lama

In Sinking Spring, Pennsylvania, on an old country road overlooking a farm, there shines a beam of light. Here lives Jane Kramer, a woman who envisions peace and happiness in our world—who not only prays for it, but visualizes it, lives it, and shares that energy with everyone she meets.

I sit in Jane's living room, and I look around. Vibrant, abstract paintings by her son Robb, an artist in New York, hang on the walls. Colorful greeting cards are propped on shelves and bookcases everywhere. The white lettering "*P-E-A-C-E*" overlays the large front window.

The phone rings. Jane ignores it. She brings me to a set of plush sofa chairs, where we both sink in. She tells me stories of her father's humor, of her mother's quiet will, of the books she loved as a child, of the miracles that have happened in her life. She shares old Irish poems. We listen to her favorite song, "Wonderful World" by Louis Armstrong. We visit her Facebook page for that frustrating article about Monsanto's latest regulatory feat, and then we watch YouTube videos of songs for peace.

The phone rings again. Jane holds a clear bag in her hand that seems to contain a piece of jewelry. She reaches for it and hands me a necklace with an opal stone pendant. The stone is meant to repel negative energy. She tells me that she has a close friend who gave her one once, and since then, she has bought several of the stones to give to her friends and family. "It can mean whatever you want it to mean," she tells me. "Carry it with you as a reminder of something important to you."

We turn back to her Facebook page, where friends have posted quotes, stories of inspiration, links to news articles and research papers. The phone rings again, and this time, Jane gets up to see who has been calling.

When she returns, I tell her she is a popular woman.

"If you looked at my calendar, you'd laugh," she smiles.

I ask her, "Do many people come to you for help with their hardships?"

Jane thinks for a moment and then responds. "Sometimes, people call me when they are upset, seeking comfort. Other times, they come for guidance or advice. But really, I do not give people answers. I try to help them become empowered to find their own answers."

She explained further. "My main purpose is to listen and read what someone is telling me. Then I feed certain parts back to that person. I essentially reflect their own thoughts back to them."

"As soon as you tell someone what to do, you become responsible for their life," she adds. "If you are doing as someone else says without believing it for yourself, it will be a lot harder to work through something than if you were to find your own answers. Each person is responsible for their own answers and their own path."

My experience in listening to Jane's story has been like this. I sit with her, we chat, and then she philosophizes with inconceivable modesty. The eloquence rests in the humble, unassuming nature of her words and phrases, and the emotion with which she utters them.

With a final thought, Jane adds, "I share what I have learned if it seems appropriate, but truly, I see my role mainly as a mirror."

***

118

Reflecting on what I have learned from Jane over the course of our time working together on this story, there are many lessons and tools that I will carry with me for the rest of my life, and for that, I am forever grateful to Jane for sharing her profound wisdom. Perhaps the most valuable—and powerful—outcome has been a newfound appreciation for my intuition. Remarkably, what Jane has accomplished is an ability to turn a gut feeling into something to be deciphered and acted upon. That is, she empowers her intuition—above all else—to be her guide. She believes it represents our "inner knowing," and it is a voice that should be nurtured, not silenced.

We have all experienced this intuitive feeling in our stomachs. Often, the most tangible manifestation of it is during a time when something doesn't *feel* "right." If there is not a rational explanation for it, we often dismiss the sensation. We tend to favor the mind's ability to analyze over the gut's ability to sense. But there is a reason why this intuition has evolved as a human trait: it is there because it has helped people evaluate opportunities, avoid danger, and make decisions that are in their best interest.

Our intuition can absolutely be a guide if we allow it to, and not simply to determine answers along a "yes-or-no" dichotomy. I have sometimes followed my gut feeling even when my mind has analyzed it differently, and I have often been rewarded for it. In my professional career, in my personal relationships and everywhere in between, I have found that I can achieve peak decision-making when I "turn up the volume" on my intuition and designate as much weight to it as my analytical thought.

***

I am one among many who have benefited from Jane's insight.

"Jane realizes that the reason she is here on earth is to share her love and energy with others," explains her friend Roe. "She has her own problems, and yet, she gets deep into ways of helping people."

Jane has an uncanny ability to use her intuition to interpret what people are feeling and where they might need help. In the words of

Jane's close friend Theresa: "Jane knows our needs before we talk about them."

A healer once asked Jane, "Do you know what you are?"

"No," Jane replied, "what am I?"

"You are *bodhisattva*."

"*Bodhi* means 'enlightened' and *sattva* means 'being,'" explained the healer. "You are motivated by wisdom and compassion. You are going through the path of suffering and you are still subject to the struggles of life, but you're at the same time free from it all. You are not caught in it. You are on a path of liberation from it—determined to be free, and also destined to help liberate others."

A friend once described the lesson she learned from Jane: "Imagine! Life is difficult, but suffering is optional?"

Surely, there is something special about Jane Kramer that is difficult to define. Her essence is captivating in an unparalleled way. People who do not even know her are drawn to her and can see this enlightened energy emanating from behind her twinkling hazel eyes and broad smile.

"Why are you buying this book? You don't need to read this," said anthropologist and author Jean Houston after Jane approached her for a book signing after one of her lectures. It was the early '90s, and Jane had picked up Jean's then-recent book, *The Possible Human,* to get signed. Jane had always admired Jean Houston, the goddaughter of Margaret Mead and an internationally renowned scholar, philosopher, and teacher whose books have gained global recognition and influenced many people. Jean began the Foundation for Mind Research in 1965 to explore and understand how cultures around the world have defined and achieved peak human potential. It is clear why this was a topic close to Jane's heart.

After Jane approached her for the book signing, Jean opened the book and signed the inside of the front cover, "To Jane—a person who is already the possible human."

Jean Houston is a woman who has given lectures around the world. She had never met Jane before. So, why had Jane stood out? Years later, after receiving her cancer prognosis, Jane would send Jean an e-mail inquiring about their encounter. Jean's response was as follows.

> *I wrote those words because I felt them. Yes, I sometimes do write something like that in my books, but only when they seem appropriate. Clearly, from the experiences you have had, you appear to be on what the Tibetan Buddhists call the "short path"—the path of intense experiences that cleanse and purify while enlightening and giving courage. Your own work in mind-body, vibrational healing is on the cutting edge of medicine and it has been my experience of those at the frontiers that we are given every opportunity to explore what we teach. There are times and we are the people and we have to rise in consciousness to be adequate stewards of this—the most challenging time in earth's history. You seem to be an agent of this process.*
>
> *—Warm regards, Jean*

Jean Houston's message rings true in Jane. Every one of us has a creative genius within our spirit that is waiting to be discovered. We have a longing to tap into our "hero's journey" and satisfy our life's purpose. To ignore this hero within us is to squander our potential as humans.

Jean believes that we are living in an extraordinary time in human history. Human civilization is awakening to higher consciousness. "When we all realize we are in this together, that will be the time that we finally know peace," Jean asserts. We all have the potential to be "agents" of this process. It is people like Jane and so many other shining stars who help light the way.

Some may call it bodhisattva, others may consider Jane to be a natural empath. That is, she senses what people are feeling without the conventional methods of information gathering. Empaths take an ability that lies latent in all of us, this ability to read energy fields, and bring it to life. Throughout her life, she has helped people work through issues by helping them uncover their own innate knowing.

"She finds it hard to dismiss someone's trouble and step back—she will more likely take it on as her own," explains her husband Ted. "As the years go by, I see more and more friends and acquaintances seeking answers from Jane. She has always been a good listener. People seem to gravitate to her as a sounding board. It's almost like she's back in her role as the guidance counselor, helping people cope."

Having found deep personal serenity, it would seem reasonable to want to shut off from the chaos of the world. But Jane does the opposite: she opens herself up to the world in intense ways. It's as if she absorbs others' troubles and despair as her own.

"No matter what you need or want to share, Jane is the first one there for me and other members of my family," said her friend Theresa.

"Jane is always willing to share with you what she knows about anything," said her friend Roe. "Sometimes, I don't want to burden her with something that I'm dealing with, but she just knows."

***

Jane affirms that, at this junction, humanity needs a higher level of consciousness. It needs—we all need—a greater sense of compassion toward our family, friends, neighbors, and strangers alike. We, as a human civilization, need an "awakening of the soul." Surely, we cannot continue on the destructive path we have been on.

But we cannot reverse direction either. So, we must find a new path toward kindness and peace, a realization that we are in this together, that we need each other and this earth in order to survive as a race.

"What we've been doing to our planet and to each other will begin to unfold in front of us," Jane perceives. "Mother nature is angry with what we've done with her." It may get worse before it gets better. But at some point, she knows that we will awaken to a higher consciousness, and we will realize that we must act on it if we wish to go on.

There is an old Cree proverb that goes: "Only when the last tree has died and the last river has been poisoned and the last fish has been caught will we realize that we can't eat money."

"What we're meant to accomplish for our planet and for each other, we haven't yet achieved," says Jane. "Greed has overpowered the need for peace and sense of community. But our consciousness is rising toward this higher vision."

***

When Jane first set out to write this book, it was difficult to know the direction it would take. There were many people in her life who advised her to write down her story. "You are meant to share it so people can learn from it," they told her.

When we began writing it down, we believed it would take the direction of a memoir. What it turned out to be is a collection of short stories infused with life's lessons and spiritual guideposts. This happened not necessarily by conscious effort, but by the nature of the information exchanged and the way that it was shared. I loved my afternoons sitting with Jane, hearing her stories, her jokes, her teachings. Chronology was rarely touched on. Rather, the stories and lessons were grouped by Jane's memories, the mood, the day.

At first, I racked my brain. *How do I tie all of the stories together?* I questioned. I went through the process of arranging them in chronological order according to the dates and chapters of her life. But in this form, the stories did not have the same flow as they did when I had first heard them.

Then—it struck me. I was following convention when the stories, the lessons, the lifetime of Jane Kramer was everything *but* conventional. When I changed my paradigm to work *against* this grain, the stories began arranging themselves naturally based on the lessons they portrayed. And perhaps a more profound realization was that, in fact, they all shared similar lessons, with only the characters and scenarios shifted around.

Trip, fall, learn, evolve.
Share the lessons you learn along the way.
Find love within yourself and emanate it outward to the world.
Remain positive, and you will attract positive things in your life.
Learn to let go of fear.
Remember that whatever is in your highest good will happen.
Your thoughts create your reality.
Live in your own truth, even if it means breaking the rules.

The following are words from several of Jane's close friends Maureen, Phil, Roe, and Janet.

My husband, Phil, informed me relatively early on in our relationship that there were important people whom he really wanted me to meet, the Kramers. He explained that Jane Kramer was his high school guidance counselor who had been, from day one, a powerful, yet gentle, accepting presence in his life who was instrumental in increasing his sense of comfort in simply being himself.

Jane has an easygoing style coupled with a keen focus on the person or task at hand. As an independent thinker, she clearly marches to her own drummer. I think it is important to note how persistent, yet funny she can be when negotiating challenging situations. She has a way of not reacting to the provocation of others while simultaneously maintaining the upper hand in the long run.

To this day, I marvel at the simplicity and effectiveness of Jane's strategy. If people won't do the right thing on their own accord, she has no problem being the gentle irritant. That's Jane.

Her spiritual quest is multifaceted and interwoven with her search to address physical challenges in alternative ways. These include treatments that are somewhat far-reaching—not your typical alternative treatments at that. From more wholesome, nontoxic remedies used in creative, atypical fashion to setting personal intention, all of her tools involve some aspect of courageous, original thinking and the assumption of personal responsibility for charting one's own healing course.

A strong mind-body connection is a key foundational component in it all. Invariably, laughter is a critical component, too. With the lighthearted sharing of treatments as well as the sharing of gifted practitioners and teachers themselves, Jane has contributed to the healing journey of those blessed to be a part of her circle.

Jane has always been a natural healer by her very presence. Through her personal journey and development, she has simply enhanced her capabilities, which have always been strongly grounded in love and respect for free will.

—Maureen

Jane Kramer started as a new guidance counselor at Governor Mifflin High School shortly before I arrived. Lucky for me, she had my half of the alphabet. The first time I sat in her office, I said nothing except a few one-word answers. I was about as withdrawn and distrustful as a person could be without being completely over the edge. Even from where I was, I could sense a benevolent, safe, and caring presence.

I started opening up slightly. By the end of the year, I was coming to Jane's office voluntarily. It was healing to feel safe and trusting with an adult with some authority. The good relationship continued through my time in high school. Jane was my favorite teacher. There were other students who were close to her, and I felt myself part of a special group.

Just as some problems had no chance of surviving her, neither did the rules under which she was supposed to work. Jane followed her own inner guide wherever it took her—the external expectations of her were followed only secondarily. She was not overtly rebellious, but when there was a conflict between the truth of what needed to be done to help a student and outer expectations, there was no doubt which would win.

Like my wife Maureen, Jane can speak truth to power and get away with it because of the force field of good intentions and truth that emanates from them. It sets them apart from the rest of us who tend to operate under the normal restrictions of diplomacy. People like Jane are unswervingly true to their mission of helping humanity one person at a time.

I was fortunate to remain close with Jane, and we have become like extended family. While never ceasing to help others, Jane has also managed to accomplish much self-healing. This has been good to see, because givers can sometimes sacrifice too much and need to take care of themselves. Jane is disciplined in her meditations and physical-healing programs. She has developed a wide network of like-minded spiritual practitioners. Some of those she has shared with us have had lasting positive effects.

—Phil

Have you ever been introduced to someone who can send vibrations to your heart and soul?

Vibrations of a strong sense of belonging, a sense of having known each other, having shared experiences together?

Have you ever been introduced to someone who is an acute observer of important things that matter to the heart?

One who seeks to find truth, who encourages you to look at yourself to see what makes your life shine?

Have you ever been introduced to someone who loves to laugh?

Who radiates strong energy waves instilling peace, joy, and harmony in the universe?

I am fortunate to be on this valuable journey with such a great friend.

—Roe

You have reinforced my belief in healing oneself, losing fear (the worst of the lot), and allowing the body to know the right thing to do when an illness strikes, whether it be physical, emotional, or mental. I am blessed that we are friends.

—Janet

I believe in the spirit of innocence, the wonder that shapes and leads us to dream. I believe that even in our darkest hour, we can take a deep breath and start all over again. Most of all, I believe in the power of love and that in the end, it will heal us all.

—Unknown

My Reflections on Writing This Memoir

Each year, around the time of my birthday, Ted and I take a trip to Ocean City, New Jersey. I see it as a time for renewal each year. The simple sensations of getting my feet in the sand at the Fifty-Ninth street beach and watching the waves roll in and out are truly grounding and bring peace to my soul. Later, on the boardwalk, I'll get Mac and Manco's pizza (which will always be the name to me), wash it down with birch beer, and finish it off with Johnson's popcorn—and then my stomach knows true joy!

This year, while down at the shore for my annual birthday trip, I opened the newspaper to a headline reading: "Everyone Has a Story to Tell." How fitting for this part of the book: my thoughts on writing the memoir. I wanted to reflect on the incredible experience I have enjoyed in sharing my story.

When I had the breast operation in 1999 and the torn rotator cuff in 2000, I took notes due to the unusual events surrounding these occasions. There were things happening that I knew I wanted to keep records on for future reference. It was only four years before writing this book that the idea of the story emerged. I was having a reading done by a medium when, in the midst of it, Rich Work came through from the other side to relay the message that he wanted my story to be told. Later, I was told that I would be writing my story with the help of a young girl.

Stefanie Angstadt was the young woman who graciously volunteered to help. What a gift she has been. I do not think she had any idea how "interesting" it was going to be, working with a free-spirited Irish

Gemini. For me, it was the perfect union because we had a close family connection, and she knew part of my story firsthand.

In 2000, Dr. Carrie had connected me with Rich Work, Ann Marie, and their healing ministry known as Symmetry. Dr. Carrie stressed to me that I needed to get Rich's book, *Awaken to the Healer Within*, because it aligned so closely with the belief system and healing paradigm that we already held close: the idea that true healing comes from within. Healing comes in many forms: physical, emotional, spiritual, financial, and social. Rich wrote many books that included powerful healing proclamations on this theme. He emphasized that the world you perceive is the world you choose to see, and there is no interpretation free from perception. In truth, your perceptions create your reality.

My friend, Carole, who is a shaman, reaffirms this concept. I, too, agree wholeheartedly with the philosophy. Visualization and setting the intention have always been a big part of my life, and they have helped shape positive perceptions, and in the end, many positive outcomes. It is incredible the new perceptions and truths that have arisen in my process of writing *Jane Against the Grain*, which is why I encourage others to write their stories, too. Reflecting on our lives brings an opportunity to gain great personal insights, as this storytelling process has truly been an awakening for me.

Rich told me that my life will touch many. Yet, as I have always believed, I am not unique in this potential. I feel the same is true for all of us; we all have the chance to connect, influence, and inspire through the sharing of our stories. It is always interesting to see how far a kind word to one person will continue to affect many others throughout the day. Many make an effort to do this. One of my friends always paid the fare for the person behind her on the Atlantic City Expressway. (Today, with EZPass, she has moved on to other ideas, but she still continues to find ways to spread the love). Some may call it "paying it forward." There are so many chances to do this in so many different ways. It is the ripple effect that begins within us and reaches outward to others.

As I was writing this memoir, and through the process, reliving my life, it became quite clear to me that out of the most difficult times often come our greatest gifts. I always knew this, but I did not realize the total picture before revisiting my life. So much gratitude fills my heart, as I now understand more fully this adventure called life.

I have always believed that the two most powerful phrases in the world are "I am" and "I choose." What are the words we will place after them? What are we choosing for ourselves? What are we asking to be?

We were in Maine when September 11 happened, and I immediately knew I wanted to be a part of the healing of our country and of our world. I was fortunate to have been introduced to a broad range of faiths at an early age at Friends Select, where we learned from people who were practicing the faith. That is where I learned about the Muslim faith and where we studied the Koran. That's why, when the news broke of the tragedy, I was saddened to hear of attacks on the Muslim world, as if the violence had somehow been tied to the faith rather than the individuals committing the act. I still wonder if the truth will ever be told, if the world will truly achieve clarity on this end. When I returned to Berks County, I called two of my close friends, and they called others. The STARS group was formed to meditate for inner peace for all throughout the world. We are still together today.

One of our women, Robin, has been paralyzed from the waist down since the spring of 1988. To know her and watch her accomplish so much has been an inspiration for all of us. Each of us in the group has experienced some extreme personal challenge. Through it all, none of us has given up the hope for world peace, nor has any of us ever uttered the words, "Why me?" I have immense respect and admiration for all of these remarkable women.

I asked them for words to describe our group. Nancy and Jane (known as "Tree") agreed that the words to characterize the group are: love, kindness, laughter, hearts that care, acceptance without judgment, inner peace, and friendship.

Mary, another member, described her experience with STARS as follows:

"The gathering of seven women to try to make sense of, and affect in a positive way, the tragedy of 9/11, began a journey for me that has been deep and profound. We have learned so much from each other's experiences in these thirteen years and have grown both individually and collectively. I am continually awed by the power we transmit when we meditate together for peace, healing, light and love for our families, our community, and our world. Seven women birthing a new world experience into being with our loving energy—amazing!"

Robin added, "STARS for me is pretty simple: harmony, love, peace, an almost indescribable feeling of camaraderie and synchronicity."

Linda said that, for her, the most remarkable aspect of STARS is "how the energy in the room changes when we are all together." She continued, "It is transformed into a healing force to the world as together we visualize a world of peaceful harmony, of loving compassion, of differences that melt away through understanding. This powerful light has the opportunity to affect all situations in all corners of the Earth. That is the power of community. That is the power of Sisters Taking a Risk Spiritually."

Finally, Roe summed it up when she described the essence of the group to be "all the quiet moments whispering prayers and meditations that have created the harmony and energy of us being among the stars in celebration."

Instead of focusing on fear and hatred —what if the world's focus would be on love and peace? It is so good to see groups all over the world promoting peace through discussion, marches and song. I saw a spiritual sticker that said, "Love makes a world they can't control." In my mind, "they" represent the forces behind the spread of fear and hatred. It is a reminder that love will conquer all.

To promote peace and unconditional love, I have often passed out blue and white bracelets. I believe in the the healing power of color, especially when setting the intent. Blue stands for peace and white for unconditional love. I got the idea when one of my friend's granddaughters was making those bracelets that are popular today. So I commissioned her in this effort to spread peace and love through the colors worn on the bracelet. They serve as a good reminder of the powerful themes that the colors signify. I am reminded of the statements of "We are all One;" and Jimi Hendrix's "When the power of love overcomes the love of power, we will know peace.

In writing this memoir, I have learned of others who have had spiritual experiences that they never shared out of concern for what others might think. While it is sad to think that these people felt they could not express their spirituality or share these special moments, it is also hopeful that many, upon hearing of this story, have been encouraged to open up and embrace these magical experiences of life. In talking to two of my older relatives about this book, I found they each had experienced their late husbands' presences in their rooms at night. One still feels her husband beside her as she goes to bed and is careful not to disturb him when she gets up each day. Another felt her husband beside her, holding her hand every night in bed, for quite a while after he passed. When she shared this story with me, she told me that one day, he was no longer there. I was so glad to be able to share experiences with her once she felt comfortable. What we were able to resolve, in the end, was that her husband was there as long as she needed him. When he left, it must have meant that she was whole enough to move on. As the author Elizabeth Kubler Ross said in one of her lectures that I was fortunate to attend in Chautauqua, New York, "God provides us with whatever or whomever we need at the time of our passing." She once said this in response to a young boy facing death who asked whether his dog would be there to greet him in heaven.

There are so many people who are sharing and writing about their spiritual experiences today, and many are surely deeper and more enlightening than my own story I share in this book. No matter how big or small, it is wonderful to see humanity feeling more comfortable about opening up to experiences that are not scientific, but rather, mystical, metaphysical, and magical. Such is what makes life extraordinary.

To all who have contributed to *Jane Against the Grain*, I want to extend my deepest gratitude. I close this book with a quote from the Dalai Lama:

"The world does not need more successful people. The world desperately needs more peacemakers, healers, storytellers, and lovers of all kinds."

To this list, I personally would add "dreamers."

With Deepest Gratitude

In gratitude to my healing community, which includes the following:

Dr. Carrie, natural metaphysical doctor, who was one of my greatest gifts; Dr. Roland Newman, who is now teaching integrated medicine to other doctors; Dr. Christopher Mclane, integrated family practitioner; Dr. Phillip A. Goedecke, Chiropractor; Dr. Len Marchinski, orthopedic surgeon who accepted my body's unusual needs; Dr. Carole LaBate, holistic dentist.

Body Workers at Pathways to Healing Wellness Center: Jane Garis, massage and energy (Reiki), Karen Gamby, cranial-sacral. Lucy Miller, lymphatic massage; Gayle Materna, retired energy/acupressure modalities; Barbara Katz, retired massage therapist.

Spiritual insights: Jean Houston, Dr. Wayne Dyer, Dr. Carrie, Ann Marie and Rich Work, Terry Ross, Michael Schuster, Carole Lipschultz and Leila Briggs. Rich, Terry, and Michael are now working from the other side. A special thank you to Dale Goodyear.

Additional Resources

Websites:

Ann Marie and Rich Work, Symmetry:
www.harmonicsinternational.com;
Dr. Alex Loyd, Ph.D., N.D.: www.TheHealingCodes.com
Tapping websites: Gary Craig, EmoFree.com;
Nick Ortner, www.thetappingsolution.com
Carole Lipschultz: www.shamanic-energy-alignment.com

References

Work, Rich. Proclamations of the Soul. 1999. Asini Publishing.

Work, Rich. Veils of Illusion. 2002. Asini Publishing.

Loyd, Alexander, N.D., Ph.D. & Johnson, Ben, M.D., D.O., M.M.D. 2004-2006. Light of Man Ministries.

Bernie S. Siegel, M.D. *Love, Medicine and Other Miracles. 1998.* William Morrow Paperbacks.

Schneider, Peter. *Einführung in die Waldorfpädogogik*, pp.20-21. 1982. Stuttgart: Klett-Cotta.

Leviton, Richard. "The Promise of Anthroposophical Medicine." East West Magazine. July 1988.

About the Authors

Jane Kramer came into this world as a free-spirited Irish Gemini. Her Celtic background nurtured her intuition and outlook on life. Her desire to help teenagers led her into the field of guidance counseling. Here, as with most things, she followed her heart rather than the rules. It is the same way she lives her life.

An uncle once told Jane she was an example of what the Irish called having "The Sight." She believes extraordinary and unbelievable life events occurred in her life to teach her the most profound of life's lessons. Her hope is that her story may encourage others to connect with their inner knowing, empowerment, and inner peace.

***

Stefanie Angstadt grew up riding a beach-cruiser bicycle around the Jersey Shore before heading off to earn a liberal arts degree at Brown University. She graduated from college and worked a corporate job in New York City for several years, but she soon began dreaming of a more natural lifestyle. She picked up and began traveling, first across the country and then across the globe, to explore farming and community food systems. She felt inspired by her grandparents' farming heritage and decided to return to her family's roots in Berks County, Pennsylvania. There, she started a small, artisan creamery and continues to passionately promote a local food community.

She is honored and grateful for the opportunity to have helped Jane share her story. She feels she has truly learned from the best teacher.

CPSIA information can be obtained at www.ICGtesting.com
Printed in the USA
BVOW04s2328071114
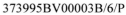

373995BV00003B/6/P